HOT BUTTONS

INSIGHT FROM GOD'S WORD ON 12 BURNING ISSUES

Compiled by Rick Bundschuh
Edited by Carol Bostrom
Illustrated by Tom Finley

Regal Books

A Division of GL Publications
Ventura, California, U.S.A.

Scripture taken from the *Holy Bible, New International Version.* Copyright ©
1973, 1978, 1984 International Bible Society. Used by permission of Zondervan
Bible Publishers.

Also quoted is *NASB—The New American Standard Bible,* copyright © The Lock-
man Foundation 1960, 1962, 1968, 1971, 1972, 1973, 1975. Used by permission;
and *KJV,* Authorized King James Version.

Library of Congress Cataloging in Publication Data

Hot Buttons.

    Contents: Clothes and culture / Rick Bundschuh — Who's in control? / Jim
Reeves — Living in a material world / Ron Sider and Dave Zercher — [etc.]
    1. Youth—Religious life. 2. Youth—Conduct of life. [1. Christian life]
I. Bundschuh, Rick, 1951-   . II. Bostrom, Carol. III. Finley, Tom, 1951-
   ill.
BV4531.2.H59   1986   248.8'3   85-32323
ISBN 0-8307-1092-2

3 4 5 6 7 8 9 / 91 90 89 88 87 86

Rights for publishing this book in other languages are contracted by Gospel
Literature International (GLINT) foundation. GLINT also provides technical
help for the adaptation, translation, and publishing of Bible study resources
and books in scores of languages worldwide. For further information, contact
GLINT, Post Office Box 477, Rosemead, California 91770, U.S.A., or the
publisher.

Contents

Introducing the Authors 5

1. Clothes and Culture 7
   Rick Bundschuh

2. Who's in Control? 17
   Jim Reeves

3. Living in a Material World 30
   Ron Sider and Dave Zercher

4. Rock 'n' Roll and the Arts 41
   David Edwards

5. Everybody Isn't Doing It! 56
   Jim Burns

6. Homosexuality 66
   Don Williams

7. Bigotry 73
   John M. Perkins

8. It's a Matter of Life and Death! 87
   Eric Pement

9. Media: Truth and Trash 99
   Tom Finley

10. Church and State 116
    David Edwards

11. Nuclear War 131
    John Hambrick

12. If I Should Die Before I Wake 142
    Ed Stewart

Introducing the Authors

Rick Bundschuh, nationally-known youth worker, is Creative Director of Youth Products at Gospel Light Publications. He has an extensive background in youth work and is a frequent speaker at camps, seminars, and churches across the country.

Jim Burns is a speaker, youth pastor, educator, counselor, and author of youth books and materials.

David Edwards is a versatile Christian musician and writer. His albums are on Myrrh and Light labels.

Tom Finley is director of Art and Promotion (Youth) at Gospel Light and is an experienced youth pastor.

John Hambrick is a writer, a musician, an experienced youth worker, and an international financial advisor.

Eric Pement is a writer for *Cornerstone Magazine* in Chicago.

John Perkins is founder and president of the John Perkins Foundation for Reconciliation and Development and of the Voice of Calvary. His books include *Let Justice Roll Down* and *With Justice for All*.

Jim Reeves is residential coordinator for the adult facility of Lincoln-Lancaster Drug Projects, Lincoln, Nebraska.

Ron Sider is professor of theology at Eastern Baptist Theological Seminary in Philadelphia, Pennsylvania. He helped to found Evangelicals for Social Action and is currently chairperson and a member of the board. He is convenor of the Unit on Ethics and Society, Theological Commission of the World Evangelical Fellowship.

Ed Stewart is a pastor, editor, and writer whose works include *Here Comes Jesus* and *A Window to Eternity*.

Don Williams is a pastor and the author of several books including one on homosexuality, *The Bond that Breaks*.

Dave Zercher is a candidate for a Master of Divinity degree at Eastern Baptist Theological Seminary. A 1983 graduate of Messiah College (Grantham, Pennsylvania), he works as administrative assistant to Ron Sider and is on the pastoral team at the Souderton (PA) Brethren in Christ Church.

1

Clothes and Culture

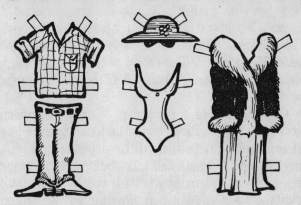

Rick Bundschuh

Blue jeans. The all-American garment. What could be a more appropriate choice for both sexes to wear if they were going to be involved in a grubby workday at a Mexican orphanage just the other side of the border?

The year was 1970, the not-so-distant past. Under the early morning overcast a score of high school students crawled into various cars and vans to make the trip across the border. They were young, devout and innocent. They had given up their Saturday to help those who could not help themselves. As they jostled their blue-jean-clad knees together over the bumpy roads they had no idea of the shock that was in store for them.

As the first vehicle pulled up to the orphanage door the students poured out of their seats, glad to stretch after the long ride. At the same time the kids of the orphanage came exploding out of the building to check out the visitors and be first in line for any "blessings" in the form of fruit or candy they might have brought with them.

One of the blue-jeaned girls approached a young boy of about ten with a large brilliantly orange tangerine. "*¿Tu quieres*" (Would you like some?) she asked in the best high school Spanish. The boy sheepishly took the tangerine and quickly disappeared. The crowd of children giggled, whispered and occasionally pointed at the American girls in their clean Levi's.

One of the guys in the group, "Chuey," was bilingual. Raised in a Puerto Rican home, he found Spanish as natural as English. He engaged the orphans in discussion immediately. It was small talk about spitting tangerine seeds and eating lemons whole. It was he who first overheard the word in a whisper. "Prostitutes" whispered one of the older orphans to another.

"What did you say?" asked Chuey in Spanish. The boy turned red and tried to hide his face down in his coat. "Where?" asked Chuey. The kid hesitated for a few moments and then jabbed a pointed finger quickly towards the girl passing out fruit from the back of a van. "Prostitute?" inquired Chuey in Spanish. "Why do you think that?"

"Pants," replied the boy. "They are all wearing pants, and everyone knows that only prostitutes wear pants."

Chuey was shocked and taken aback at the obvious cultural valley he had just fallen into. He tried to explain that in the United States most girls wear pants at least some of the time. He was not sure that his explanation was being received. These kids had never been north of the border. All they knew of what life was like was what they had seen in the little *colonia* or colony in which they lived. Chuey even noticed the neighbors standing in the doorways and pointing. He could imagine them saying to one another, "What are all those prostitutes doing at the orphanage?"

Chuey went to the leader of the group with the revelation. The leader was surprised and then quiet for a moment. Then he asked all the girls wearing pants to climb into the cars. Their workday was over but their horror was just beginning as they were told that they had been mistaken for benevolent hookers. They waited on the other side of the border for their male counterparts to finish working.

The next workday planned by the group was accompanied by a large announcement that said "All girls must wear dresses."

This incident may strike you as humorous, unfair, sexist, petty, ignorant or just silly. Regardless of how you feel about blue jeans being the attire of prostitutes, it is clear that clothing styles communicate different things to different people.

CLOTHING THROUGH THE CENTURIES

The first recorded clothing was a quickly assembled array of fig leaves, cheap but tough to put through the washing machine (see Gen. 3:7). The clothes of most of the people in the Bible consisted of square-cut cloth of linen or wool. The basic costume was unisex, but the differences between men's and women's clothing were evident in designs and decorations woven into the ladies' robes. Clothes made of rare materials such as silk were considered the prized possessions of the wealthy. Most people had few if any changes of garment. The status of a person was often indicated by the kind of clothes he or she was privileged to wear.

The Bible does not make a big deal out of clothes. It warns us that members of one sex should not go around dressed like the other sex. (See Deut. 22:5. Even though there was a basic sameness to the clothing of men and women in Bible times, there was enough of a difference to be able to tell.) Scripture also warns us not to put all of our energy into dressing up the outside but rather to put the energy into adorning the inside (see 1 Pet. 3:3,4).

Even though the Bible is relatively quiet about clothing, many Christians are not. In many churches the pulpit rings with condemnation of various types of fashion and hairstyles. Christian homes often erupt into full-blown wars over hair, makeup or clothing. If the Bible is so quiet why do Christians make so much noise? The answer is not always an easy one but it may have to do with some of the following observations.

CLOTHING COMMUNICATES

For most western people clothes have far more than a practical function of warmth and protection. They are a costume. They are a uniform. They say what role you are playing, what side you are on or what ideas you subscribe to. Even bizarre-looking people tend to look similarly bizarre. Some say they are trying to be different but how come all the different people look so oddly similar? Why is it someone who wants to be different isn't really different?

In the selection of our costume we make subtle or obvious statements. We identify ourselves to one degree or another.

Some kids in the early sixties loved to wear replicas of

iron crosses around their necks. Most of them didn't really have a reason for doing it other than it drove their folks crazy to see their offspring wearing the symbol of a nation that they fought against in World War II. The crazier it drove the parents the more cool it was to wear the dumb things. The main reason that most kids wore the crosses was that other kids did it and it showed they were really independent of their parents' values—even if they were good values.

Clothing is more costume than covering in western cultures. Because of this, if a person sees the values and ideas of something evil (such as Nazi fascism) being represented by the costume of another (especially if that person is a member of the same household or church) it is no wonder that there is a loud outcry of protest. (To get a clear picture of what parents may feel, try to imagine how you would feel if your father decided he wanted to dress and look like Adolf Hitler. You sure wouldn't want to be seen goose-stepping with him in public.)

Of course the difficulty with labeling a costume is that some of the darkest and most evil people in the world wear nice suits and look conservatively clean-cut. If we were to label a costume selfish, greedy, or merciless what would it look like?

Some people wear costumes that are designed to stimulate others sexually or to heighten the wearer's sensuality. Some wear such clothing in ignorance, others wear it with intent. The result is usually the same: it attracts the opposite sex for the wrong reason. In some ways this is much like the old trick of taping a "kick me" sign to some poor sucker's back and then watching the person get booted down the hall. Except those who dress to be sexy often place the "kick me" (or "use me") signs on their own backs. Their costume is the surface fruit of a much deeper problem that needs to be dealt with by God's love and compassion.

Some people wear clothing to show off their economic status and all-around good taste. They generally spend most of their time impressing each other since the average toad on the street doesn't give a rip if a coat costs $1000 or $20. Again, these people are almost to be pitied rather than scorned since their lives are so bankrupt of character they must get their worth out of at least looking successful.

CLOTHING AND STEWARDSHIP

There is another element that comes into play when a Christian begins to wrestle with the issue of clothing and culture. That element is called stewardship, or the right use of money. Clothes cost money, sometimes big money. Christians must deal not only with the desire to stay in "style" culturally but with the fact that each dollar they have is a gift from God to be used wisely and compassionately. This should cause Christians to ask themselves questions that those who do not know Christ seldom ask. "Do I need this pair of shoes badly enough to spend $60 on them?" "Should I sink hundreds of dollars into an outfit that I will probably wear only once?" "Should I buy this outrageously styled and colored shirt knowing full well that it has a very short life expectancy for being stylish—and a very large price tag?"

These considerations cover not only clothes but jewelry, makeup and anything else that is dangled, draped or drilled on our body. How much gold and how many jewels a Christian should own and display is too complex a question to dive into in a chapter on clothes, but it is one of those thorny issues that *needs* to be handled by every believer who is seriously investing God's money towards them.

CLOTHING AND PARENTS

Another factor in clothes has to do with the feelings and wishes of parents. Since the Bible is clear that we are to obey our parents, the apparel of a Christian high school student must pass the permission test of the family structure (see Col. 3:20). This should not mean a license for parents to frustrate the independence and decision-making ability of their offspring (Scripture has something to say about that as well—see Col. 3:21), but it does mean that if after a loving and understanding dialogue there is not an agreement on wearing the zebra striped spandex shorts to the church service the child is to bow to the wisdom of the parent.

A MATTER OF MODESTY

Another margin or fence for Christians in the area of clothes comes from the teaching of Scripture encouraging modesty (see 1 Tim. 2:9). The difficulty is that this fence seems to move and twist depending on the time and culture we find ourselves in. For instance, we would be outraged if a man showed up for dinner wearing a long wig, makeup, a ruffled blouse, silk pantaloons (tight pants), and stockings. It is completely inappropriate attire. But it was the way true gentlemen such as Mozart, Washington, and Jefferson dressed when going out.

We might think the Christians of a South American jungle tribe immodest for their lack of clothing in the tropical heat: they would think us silly for our abundance of clothing in the same heat.

Great-great-Grandma would have raced to an early

grave if she could have seen what her descendants would one day consider modest apparel at the beach. In fact, modesty even varies according to the setting within the culture. What one wears to swim in is not considered modest or appropriate if worn to a concert downtown.

Of course this is the culture that we live in, and at this writing there are still things that are considered immodest for people to wear. Christians must be conscious of this "moving line" of modesty and do their best to stay within it for the place and times they live in.

AVOID OFFENDING

Another margin by which the costuming of a Christian must be hemmed in is the idea that we are to so love our fellow Christians (and people in general) that we do nothing that will interfere with their spiritual well-being (see 1 Cor. 10:32). This means being sensitive to what genuinely offends people and cripples their walk with God. This does not mean that we are to be particularly worried about wearing things that others do not personally care for. For example, I do not care for polyester clothing. I think it looks dumb and tacky. This is simply my opinion. I am right as long as *I* don't wear polyester clothes. I am wrong once I start telling *you* not to. You would do better to ignore me and let me grow up by figuring out that I cannot and should not impose my personal tastes on you.

With so many conditions and things to think about it may seem easier just to chuck it and wear whatever you want whenever you want to. It may be easier but it does not help us to grow and stretch in our Christian lives. It may be that we really do need to stop and rethink our "costume." Is the message we give really what we want to say? Is the costume worth the hassles in our family relationships? Is the money we spend going towards things that will matter in eternity?

WHAT IS REALLY IMPORTANT?

Probably one of the saddest things about clothing and our culture is that for many the exterior, the costume, the hair, the makeup, and the "look" are tremendously important.

It is not wrong to take care of what God has given us and to do the best job we can sprucing up our "earthly temple." Obviously a clean, fresh-smelling person is a much nicer person to be around than someone with sewer breath and the odor of mildew seeping from his or her clothing. At the same time, we must get our perspective correct. The clothes will rot, the hair will thin, the body will sag regardless of what we do to try to stop it. Time and gravity play the same brutal tricks on all things made of flesh. If our lives are invested in externals we are in dire straits. Our energy should first be directed toward the inside, to make us presentable in character. The excess of that energy should then spill over into the cosmetics of life.

Jesus Himself said, "A man's life does not consist in the abundance of his possessions" (Luke 12:15). He also asked the rhetorical question, "What can a man give in exchange for his soul?" (Mark 8:37). The answer to that question might very well be: "Money, fashion, style and the longing to be hip in the eyes of others." Our Lord also had a stern warning: "Do not store up for yourselves treasures on earth, where moth and rust destroy, and where thieves break in and steal" (Matt. 6:19). The horrible truth is that for many people—even some who call themselves Christians—their treasure hangs in the closet, rests on shoe racks and lies sleeping in jewelry boxes. Such treasure gives a false hope, a temporary feeling of being somebody while the somebody we were created to be lies unexplored.

Ultimately it will make little difference to God what we look like on the outside, but it will make an incredible difference to Him what we are like on the inside.

For those struggling or battling with clothes, hair, jewelry, makeup and the rest of the trappings of our culture, we have the biblical guidelines of modesty, care for the spiritual well-being of others, obedience to parents, stewardship of money, and the desire to work on the inner person with greater urgency and care than we work on the outer appearance.

2
Who's in Control?

Jim Reeves

One of the hottest buttons facing our society is the use and abuse of intoxicants, a category which includes drugs and alcohol. The material in this chapter is designed to provide factual information about these substances along with biblical guidelines regarding their use.

WHAT DRUGS ARE AND WHAT THEY DO

What is a drug? It has been called a powerful substance that can change one's mood, perception, or way of thinking. Alcohol does this, and so does cocaine, but what about soda pop? Can it change one's mood or feelings? Can it change one's perception or senses? Or can it change one's ability to think clearly? Soda pop contains caffeine, a stimulant drug served in a mild dose, and sugar. Is sugar a drug? It strongly affects the body, and experts say it affects mental function and creates hyperactivity. How about chocolate? It contains sugar, along with a natural chemical substance related to caffeine called coca. We could go on with the list. What then is a drug? Is it heroin, cocaine, marijuana, and alcohol only? Should we include coffee, colas, and candy? According to our definition a drug can be almost any substance, and these substances cannot always be avoided. Without a doubt, we use drugs of all kinds on a daily basis. Chemical substances like caffeine in colas and coca in chocolate are in such small doses they seem to harm no one. Over-the-counter medications for colds and congestion contain small amounts of mood and mind altering drugs, but with precautions they are OK for most people to use. Doctor's prescriptions are stronger over-the-counter medications, but we count on the physician's judgment not to over-medicate us. Street drugs seem scarey because everyone in authority says they are dangerous to use. We need to know what these chemicals can do to our bodies.

Alcohol and Other Sedatives

Alcohol is the most popular liquid intoxicant in the world, consumed by millions of people on a daily basis. Alcoholic beverages have been known for thousands of years. Noah discovered their effects and got drunk not long after leaving the ark (see Gen. 9:20,21). Old Testament writers and ancient historians have recorded testimonies of the good and ill effects of drinking Alcohol is known for its sedative effect on the body; in small doses it can: help reduce stress in the body; promote health and digestion (see 1 Tim. 5:23); decrease heart attack risks (ask your doctor); and help in the relief of pain (see Prov. 31:6,7). In large doses over time alcohol has been observed to produce drunkenness and the destruction of cells in vital organs of our body. You may have heard all about the destructive effects of alcoholism on relationships and on the body.

Alcohol is an interesting intoxicant to learn about since people use it so much. Experts in the field of chemical substances call alcohol a sedative or depressant. At first glance alcohol does not seem like a sedative. In low doses it makes people feel relaxed, happy, cheerful, and very lively. At this point the alcohol has lowered the person's sensitivity to outside stimulation. A person feels less inhibited or restrained from behaving according to the way he or she feels inside. Watch some people you know who drink a little and see if they allow themselves to be happy or playful. The more one drinks the more relaxed one feels. At some point one gets drunk. Drunkenness robs the person of the ability to speak clearly and to walk with steady legs. Continuous drinking at one time eventually leads to a complete loss of consciousness. Does this sound like anything you have observed at parties where your friends have become drunk?

Aside from alcohol, there are other chemicals that act as sedatives in the body. Doctors use tranquilizers, anesthetics, and pain relievers to help their patients feel less pain and cope with their illnesses. The effects of drugs like Valium, Librium, and other downers are similar to those of alcohol. Doctors also use narcotics to help sedate people, but these substances have a far more powerful effect on the body.

Narcotics

A narcotic dulls the senses and causes a person to sleep. Narcotics cause sedative effects similar to those of the drugs in the previous category. Narcotics do more than sedate the nervous system (like depressants), they sedate the sensors in the brain, thus creating a high sense of euphoria. Narcotic drugs like Percodan, Percoset, Darvoset, and morphine are used by physicians to help their patients feel less pain while the body is healing. Opium is the parent plant of all narcotic drugs. We may suspect that the gall which was added to wine during the time of Christ was a narcotic drug because of its potential to relieve the pain experienced on the cross (see Matt. 27:34). Even though narcotics are effective with pain, they are also highly addictive. Doctors prescribe them with caution and try to keep their patients from becoming dependent on them. Unfortunately many do. On the street, narcotic drugs like opium, heroin, codeine, and morphine are potent chemicals that leave a person open to dependency. Whether a narcotic is prescribed or not, medical authorities suggest following these rules with narcotic drugs:

1. Use them only for severe physical pain or discomfort.

2. Never inject a narcotic into the body for nonmedical purposes. Such usage can leave you open to repeated experiences and can lead to dependency on the substance.

3. Even when a narcotic provides extreme pleasure the first time, there is no guarantee you will experience a repeat performance a second time. Addiction can happen when a person continues to pursue that elusive pleasure.

Stimulants

Doctors also use drugs that elevate a person's mood. Many people use stimulants every day. You may have seen a TV commercial picturing a scene much like a police chase. Two guys in a car chase a motorcyclist through the city. The passenger in the car is obviously nervous and worried as his partner goes through hairpin turns and several near-misses. The punch line to the commercial is "Life is stimulating enough for some people, so for them we have made caffeine free _____ cola." Obviously this cola company knew the stimulating effect that caffeine has on the body's system. Stimulants of all kinds activate, energize and make a person more alert. Caffeine in colas or coffee is in small doses compared to prescription medications or street drugs. Doctors prescribe anti-depressant drugs to stimulate the body's system. Stimulants are found in cold medications to offset the drowsiness experienced from its use. Speed, crank, uppers are just a few of the slang words used on the street to describe stimulants. The most controversial drug in this category is cocaine, which is a derivative of the leaves of the coca plant. Repeated use leads to dependence, which becomes an expensive habit to maintain.

Psychedelics

L.S.D., Mescaline, Magic Mushrooms, M.D.A. are some of the chemicals called psychedelics or hallucinogens. They are not prescribed by doctors but are found only on the street. Some users of these drugs claim they can explore the mind and probe the origins of religious feelings. Nonusers are fearful of these drugs because they consider them dangerous chemicals capable of driving people to insanity or suicide. As powerful as these substances are, one's state of mind and mood contribute a great deal to the outcome of one's "trip." Visions and hallucinations come from within one's mind, and these drugs unleash whatever lies deep within the mind. This is not to say that you should use these drugs on the basis of these descriptions. Psychedelics are powerful chemicals that can cause great emotional trauma and some physical ill effects.

Marijuana

The final chemical for this discussion is marijuana. Marijuana is as old a drug as time itself, dating back as long as alcohol. It is the product of the hemp plant, Cannabis sativa, which provides fiber used in making rope, an edible plant, an oil, and a medicine. The intoxicating part comes from the sticky resin exuded by the female plant. Historians through the centuries have described several instances where Assyrians and Persians used hemp-type plants for intoxicating purposes.

Marijuana has a unique characteristic. It can act like a sedative and a stimulant almost at the same time. It can be abused more easily than psychedelics can because it can be used more frequently and continuously through a variety of different activities in one day. Since it has the ability to heighten one's perceived enjoyment in activities, it tends to encourage continued use. People sometimes suggest that smoking pot leads to heroin or L.S.D. usage. Although marijuana has no chemical effect that could push a person to use these "harder" drugs, using marijuana can introduce a person to the experience of using drugs and can make the use of drugs seem more familiar and comfortable.

Marijuana does irritate the respiratory tract, and does create the same potential problems as tobacco. The main danger of smoking marijuana is that it will get away from you. Continued use will develop a habit of usage that will be hard to break. Every activity can become associated with smoking marijuana so that you no longer control your smoking but your smoking controls you.

HOW TO RELATE TO DRUGS

We have spent a lot of time looking at what various drugs do to our bodies. You may be asking yourself, "What drugs are OK for me to use? When is it OK to use them? Does God say anything about using drugs of any kind?" The Bible does give some guidelines for the use of intoxicants. We will consider these in four major categories: social customs; ignorance and curiosity; avoiding problems; and medical purposes.

Social Customs: All of us come from various social and cultural backgrounds. You may have friends who drink wine as part of their meals. To them it is a family tradition to drink on social occasions. Other families will not touch any kind of drink; some condemn anyone who does. Family traditions are a part of what makes us all different. But we need to put our family traditions aside long enough to look at some passages from the Bible.

The Bible does not give a blanket rule forbidding drinking. It does say that we are not to get drunk nor associate with drunks. Paul tells us in Ephesians 5:18 that we are not to be drunk to the point of debauchery. What that means is we are not to indulge ourselves in drinking to the point that it harms us. When drinking too much leads to poor and foolish choices at a party, then obviously a person is harming himself or herself and others. In addition, the same verse tells us to be controlled by the Holy Spirit. Those who choose to drink need to ask, "Who's in control? Alcohol or God?" And they need to remember that Christians' bodies are God's temple, bought at the price of

Jesus' death (see 1 Cor. 6:19,20).

Too much wine or beer leaves us in a position to make poor choices and can lead us astray (see Prov. 20:1). Paul points out in Galatians 5:21 that drunkenness is an act of our sinful nature which we are not to be a part of. In Romans 13:13 Paul portrays drunkenness as an act of sin and darkness. Getting drunk is not wise.

The Bible even hits hard on associating with drunkards. Some fatherly advice comes from Proverbs 23:20,21, which says not to associate with drunkards or gluttons. The association may not lead to drinking, but the picture points out that this kind of group goes nowhere. Peter shows us in 1 Peter 4:3,4 that drunkenness is associated with the old nature and other worldly practices of the past. "Put away the past" is Peter's point, "including your associates and friends who get drunk." Paul goes even farther to say that any professing Christian who drinks heavily is not to be associated with by other Christians (see 1 Cor. 5:11). A drunkard who says he is a Christian should not be allowed to eat at your dinner table, so Paul says. What a statement!

What about drinking to be sociable? Did not Jesus drink on social occasions? (Some Christians believe that He drank non-alcoholic wine.) As mentioned earlier, drinking is not condemned in the Bible, drunkenness is. A good example of drinking is Jesus's visit to the wedding in Cana (see John 2:1-11). Everyone present at the wedding was there to socialize and celebrate the good fortune of the bridegroom. The environment was just right for everyone to have a good time, but social customs most likely prevented over-use.

Not long after Jesus arrived they ran out of wine. It wine were wrong for the party He would not have created more. His decision to create wine for the party apparently showed His acceptance of the use of a potential intoxicant for a socially acceptable celebration. On other occasions, such as the Last Supper, He also drank wine.

The other side of the sociability coin, however, is our obligation to other people. Paul wrote, "So whether you eat or drink or whatever you do, do it all for the glory of God. Do not cause anyone to stumble, whether Jews, Greeks, or the church of God" (1 Cor. 10:31,32). One Christian may be able to use a moderate amount of wine with no problem. But if another Christian, seeing the first one use wine, decides to try it and gets drunk or strays away from God, the first Christian has caused the second to stumble. Similarly, if a Christian is trying to win a friend to Christ, and the friend feels that Christians should not drink, then the Christian friend should avoid drinking in order not to put up a barrier to the other's conversion.

Ignorance and Curiosity

Maybe you or someone you know has experienced a situation similar to the one that follows. John gets off the bus from school with his buddies and they begin to walk home together. They have known each other for several years. Jerry pulls a joint (a marijuana cigarette) out of his pocket and motions for everyone to follow him into a nearby alley. John never before knew that Jerry smoked pot. It looks interesting enough, and all the guys want to smoke it. John thinks for a moment about his parents and how they always tell him to stay away from any form of drugs. Even his pastor has condemned the stuff. But John decides to try it along with his friends. He feels some apprehension about it and is a little nervous. *"Wow!* What a feeling!" he thinks to himself. He feels good and relaxed after a few drags, and at the same time he is experiencing some anxiety, even paranoia. Everyone is sitting in a circle smiling at each other. Once in a while someone looks over his shoulder in case of a bust.

Suddenly a loud noise comes from the other side of a nearby fence. Without checking it out, everyone takes off as fast as they can in different directions. John gets home almost out of breath. Looking in the mirror he sees that his eyes are dilated (the pupils are open) more than usual. "Boy, am I scared!" he thinks, as he begins to look out the window for cops. Every noise and sound seems heightened and he feels more frightened than he has ever felt before. What caused the intense fear in John? How could John have avoided this experience?

As the story pointed out, ignorance of what a drug can and will do to one's system is not wise. A serious problem when using anything in ignorance is panic. You may know someone who was slipped a drug without his or her knowledge. The unsuspecting person may have experienced panic, anxiety, fear, and personal doubt of his or her sanity during the experience. Taking a substance you suspect is a drug just because your friends say it is cool can produce fear, anxiety, and paranoia because you don't know what to expect and you may have some fear of getting caught. "Bad trips" on a hallucinogenic or narcotic can be caused by a panic reaction to the drug. Ignorance of after-effects can cause problems as well. Having a good experience turn bad (crashing) can produce depression and an extreme desire to get back to the high. Depression is a common reaction to loss of a good experience. If someone does not realize this fact they may associate the depression with some other problem and use drugs to avoid the emotional pain. Our curiosity urges us to find out about things in life. Experience is often the best teacher—but not in the area of drugs. Read what you can about all kinds of drugs, and learn what you can from others who know.

Remember, using anything out of ignorance can be dangerous.

Avoiding Problems

People use drugs for various reasons. Staff people in drug and alcohol rehabilitation centers find most of those reasons are to avoid problems or issues in life. Some areas are: avoiding conflicts with friends or parents; avoiding feelings of pain over loss of a relationship; destroying oneself because of a poor self-image; "consumable courage" just to function on a day to day basis. These are extreme issues of course, but these issues don't just happen. They are worked up to, built from small seeds of guilt, doubt, hurt, anger, fear, loneliness, boredom and so on. These seeds can grow to full problems when left unresolved.

When people decide to use a substance to avoid facing problems in life, then they are allowing that substance to be in charge of their lives. Dependency on a chemical substance to avoid problems is a complete loss of freedom. God is left out of the picture. This is not what God wants for us. For a Christian to use a chemical substance in order to avoid problems means he or she is giving up letting God control the problem. Peter says it well: "Cast all your anxiety on him because he cares for you" (1 Pet. 5:7). Paul points out in Philippians 4:6,7 that we are to be anxious (worried or fearful) about nothing, but in any and every circumstance take our problems to God in prayer. God will provide us with His peace. God wants to be the controlling force in our lives. We are God's temple and His possession (see 1 Cor. 6:19,20). Any and all use of His property is to be for His honor and glory.

Medical Purposes

Doctors prescribe drugs to help people with their illnesses. The Bible makes a few medical recommendations of its own when it comes to intoxicants. King Lemuel received excellent advice from his mother regarding the use of alcohol; she told him that a person in leadership should avoid drinking as much as possible (see Prov. 31:4,5). Craving alcohol leads to poor judgment and corruption. The passage goes on to say that wine does have some medicinal use. A person who is perishing, or in great pain physically, needs something to relieve the hurt (see vv. 6,7). Wine does have the ability to numb the emotional and physical pain of a suffering person. Drinking even helps someone forget for a time (see v. 7). Doctors don't use wine for these purposes anymore, but they used to do so.

Paul may have talked with his own physician, Dr. Luke, about Timothy's stomach disorder and frequent ailments, for we find the apostle advising the younger man to use some wine for his stomach (see 1 Tim. 5:23). This medical use could have been in order to aid his digestion or to relieve some pain he experienced in his body. The Romans used gall, possibly an opium drug, to relieve the pain of those on the cross (see Matt. 27:34). The good Samaritan used wine with oil in order to treat the wounds of the stranger (see Luke 10:34).

RESPONSIBLE USE OF DRUGS

In looking at intoxicants we have found that we are to use them responsibly. A philosophy for responsible use might include the following points:

1. We should recognize what substances are drugs and be aware of what they can do to our bodies.

2. We should be able to separate ourselves from a drug. Dependency and addiction to any substance are sure signs of a lack of responsibility.
3. We should be conscious of any adverse effects of drugs upon our health or behavior.
4. We should always use our bodies and our minds to glorify and please God.

As you think about your own use of drugs, keep these points in mind so you can use drugs responsibly.

3

Living in a Material World

Ron Sider and Dave Zercher

Brad is uptight. The night of the Junior-Senior Prom has finally arrived, and like most teenaged prom-goers, Brad is hoping that this night will be the beginning of something wonderful. For months he has been dying to go out with Jenny, and now "their" time has finally come. Not about to take any chances, Brad has decided that it is wise to go all out. Yes, he realizes that $15 is a lot of money to spend on a corsage that will wilt by midnight, but he figures Jenny is worth it. Ditto for the $70 tux rental, even though it needs to be returned on Monday. Sure, he could have worn his suit, but special nights call for special expenditures. Besides, Brad reminds himself, this *is* a once in a lifetime thing.

Jenny, too, is uptight. Although she doesn't know Brad too well, her friends have told her that he is quite a catch. Thus, like Brad, Jenny has decided that tonight is no night to cut corners. "I hope he likes my hair," she thinks as she eyes her $40 perm in the mirror. "And I hope he likes my new dress too." The dress she bought for the choir concert was definitely cuter, but Brad is in the choir and he had probably already seen it. And, of course, her parents were more than glad to spring for a new one. Special nights call for special expenditures, they had assured her. Besides, this *is* a once in a lifetime thing.

Brad and Jenny are not real people, but their situation is far from imaginary. Most American teenagers—both Christians and non-Christians—have stood in their sneakers at one time or another. There's no denying that we want to impress those who impress us, and one of the easiest ways to do that is by looking good. But in this day of rapidly changing fashions, looking good is expensive. If we want to be "in," we must literally be willing to pay the price.

Most Americans don't give this matter a second thought. Even as teenagers, we are more than willing to pay the price of being accepted by the crowd, whether that means spending $45 for a pair of sunglasses or $60 for a designer you-name-it. What we fail to realize, however, is that paying the price is not an option for many people in our world. While we worry about looking good, many people in our world worry about the source of their next meal . . . and survival itself. Furthermore, although the Bible calls us to many things, the call to impress others by our material possessions is not one of them. So where does that leave us? We have a desire—a very natural desire—

for nice things, yet the world around us starves. Let's take a closer look.

THE LONG AND THE SHORT OF IT

We don't need to be economists to know that America is an affluent nation. We pride ourselves on being industrious and prosperous, and our egos are bruised when another country outdoes us on the economic market. Yet, sometimes we are guilty of taking too much credit for ourselves. It is foolish—even sinful—to ignore God's role in our prosperity. He has blessed our nation with fertile farmland, a favorable climate, and an abundance of natural resources. Exactly *why* our country has been so blessed, we don't know. We certainly haven't earned these gifts; we do, however. accept them with thankful hearts.

Occasionally, we even pause to remember those who are "less fortunate" than we are. "Less fortunate" is a polite way to avoid saying the words "starving to death." We can avoid the words, but we cannot ignore the facts. The evening news brings famine victims into our living rooms just when we are sitting down for supper. And when the newscast breaks away for a commercial, we are urged to send our dollars to the Peace Corps or the Red Cross for famine relief. Then, just as we are about to lose our appetite, Mom reminds us that there's a starving child in Africa who would love the peas and carrots we left on our plate. It's enough to make us feel guilty for having what we have!

Soon, however, most of us are able to push those images from our minds. It's much more fun to discuss Friday night's ball game than it is to discuss Ethiopia. And it's much more fun to shop at the mall than it is to think of how we might help those we don't even know and probably never will. Yet our avoidance of the issue does not solve the problem. It's sad but true that 40,000 small children die from starvation, malnutrition, and related diseases every single day.[1] Of course, there *is* hope. The United Nations Children's Fund estimates that for every hundred dollars it spends, one child's life can be saved.[2] Unfortunately, UNICEF's $300 million annual budget does not go very far toward eliminating this crisis. On the other hand, Americans spent enough money ($23 *billion*) on soft drinks in 1984 to save 230 million hungry children, 15 times the number that actually died. And we bought enough chewing gum to save 14 million more.

The situation is clear: In the United States, we buy products we don't even need, but in many parts of our world, people need things they can't even afford. We hurt for those who are less fortunate, and we do what we can. We hold walkathons, bikeathons, and starvathons. We take special offerings; we even buy record albums proclaiming "We Are the World!" We would never dream, however, of trading places with the less fortunate or even diminishing the style of life to which we've grown accustomed. In fact, this runs counter to the American way of life—a way of life which tells us the only honorable direction on the ladder of success is UP!

JESUS AND MONEY

As far as we know, Jesus never went to a prom. He never drank Coca-Cola, He never chewed bubble-gum, He never rented a tux, and He certainly never wore designer jeans. But He did have money and so did His disciples. So, despite the fact that Jesus lived 2000 years ago in a culture far, far away, He had to deal with the same issues we do today. And as one reads the Gospels, it doesn't take long to discover that money was one of His favorite topics of discussion.

So what did Jesus say about money? There are two ways to go about answering this question. First, we can rely upon others to tell us what Jesus said. This is the easy way to get an answer. But this method has a definite shortcoming: Depending upon who we listen to, we might hear conflicting stories. For example, one person might tell us that wealth is God's blessing upon hard-working people. Another person might tell us that wealth is actually a curse and that poverty is God's true blessing. Some preachers say that God wants us to be rich; other preachers say that God prefers we remain poor. So, as we can see, letting others tell us what Jesus said about money may seem simple, but it can get quite confusing.

The better way to go about solving this problem is to look at the Scriptures themselves. In these few pages, it is impossible to examine everything Jesus said about money. Yet, as we study the Gospels, a number of overriding principles begin to grab our attention:

1. *As Christians, our primary allegiance is to God.* Nowhere is this more clearly spelled out than in Matthew 6:24: "No one can serve two masters," says Jesus. "You cannot serve both God and Money." Apparently the rich ruler (see Luke 18:18-30) wanted to do just that. He wanted to inherit eternal life, yet he was not willing to trade his earthly treasures for a heavenly treasure. It is easy for us who have possessions, no matter how few, to sympathize with the rich ruler. We feel even better when we realize that Jesus did not tell everyone He met to sell all they had. In fact, Jesus never even said that material things are necessarily evil. However, His words clearly indicate that material possessions are dangerous when they

become overly important to a person. "Indeed, it is easier for a camel to go through the eye of a needle than for a rich man to enter the kingdom of God" (Luke 18:25).

2. *Christians should seek the kingdom of God rather than worry about worldly possessions.* In Luke 12:13-21, Jesus tells the parable of the rich fool, a farmer who decides to hoard grain for his future consumption. When the farmer's future is cut short, his foolishness becomes apparent—it's hard to eat when you are dead! Jesus follows this illustration with a blunt message to His disciples: "Do not worry about your life, what you will eat; or about your body, what you will wear . . . . But seek his [God's] kingdom, and these things will be given to you as well" (Luke 12:22,31). No doubt the disciples found these words as difficult to follow as we do!

3. *God exhibits a special concern for the poor.* Psalm 140:12 states that "the Lord secures justice for the poor and upholds the cause of the needy." It's evident that God expects His people to exhibit the same concern. In Matthew 25:31-46 Jesus indicates that He actually identifies with those who are hungry and homeless. On the other hand, those who are blessed with the resources to assist the hungry and the homeless are condemned when they fail to provide assistance. Jesus blasts their insensitivity: "I tell you the truth, whatever you did not do for one of the least of these, you did not do for me" (Matt. 25:45).

God's special concern for the poor is again emphasized in the parable of the rich man and Lazarus (see Luke 16:19-31). The rich man lives his whole life in luxury; Lazarus is forced to live off the scraps that fall from the rich man's table. Although the parable never mentions which of the two men is more spiritual, God's favor is clearly indicated at their respective deaths. Whereas the beggar is carried to Abraham's side, the rich man is tormented in hell. Lazarus, who received no assistance from the rich man during his life, has a name that literally means "the one whom God has helped." Thus, Jesus is contrasting God's special concern for poor Lazarus with the rich man's lack of concern.

4. *"Love your neighbor" is a command, not an option.* The second greatest commandment, according to Jesus, is: "Love your neighbor as yourself" (Matt. 22:39). Obviously, Jesus is not speaking of the type of love we see on soap operas or the late movies. Nobody loves himself or herself in that way! Rather, Jesus is commanding us to love our neighbors in the same way as we love ourselves—by actively caring for their emotional, spiritual, and physical well-being. This certainly includes battling the problem of hunger and poverty.

Jesus is careful to point out that "loving our neighbor" is far more than just loving our friends. The parable of the Good Samaritan (see Luke 10:25-37) illustrates the fact that anybody in need—even an enemy—is our neighbor. At the completion of this well-known parable, Jesus supplies His listener with a simple plan for action: "Go and do likewise."

HOW MUCH IS OK?

It is evident, then, that Jesus was not silent on economic issues. He looked around at the prevailing culture and saw that people's priorities were pretty mixed up. He had to make a statement. Sometimes, however, we wish that His advice was a little more specific. Instead of "You cannot serve both God and Money," we wish He had said: "It's OK to have three pairs of jeans, but only one of them can be Jordache." Or maybe, "Yes, two trips to McDonald's per month are permissible, but instead of going a third time, give $5 to the World Hunger Fund."

Fortunately, however, Jesus knew the difference between human beings and robots. Part of the excitement—and responsibility—of being human is making our own decisions and then living with the consequences. And although there is plenty of material in the Bible to give us guidance in how we should spend our money, in the end the specific choices rest with us.

The Bible isn't alone, however, in trying to help us decide what to buy. The media—radio, television, magazines—are continually attempting to influence our buying habits through manipulative advertising. In fact, it is estimated that the average American teenager has watched 350,000 TV commercials before leaving high school.[3] Many of these commercials inform us that we need a certain product which, just minutes before, we didn't even know existed. Creating desire is what advertising is all about, and the advertising establishment goes too far, fostering within us a compulsion to be in style. For example, one company markets its clothing with the slogan: "We're the difference between being 'dressed' and 'well-dressed.'" Another advertisement encourages us to "make a career out of being in style."

Our peers, too, are a major influence upon our spending habits. Nobody wants to be an oddball. If all of our friends have high-top leather Nikes, it's hard to be content wearing low-cut canvas sneakers, even though they sell for one-fourth the price. Likewise, it may be that a pair of cut-off shorts serves the same purpose as a pair of name brand shorts, but everyone knows that cut-offs aren't nearly as "cool." Let's face it—at one time or another, all of us have tried to impress others with our possessions. And, of course, it's only natural to enjoy receiving compliments on a new blouse or a new cycle. But there has to be a limit . . . doesn't there? In a world with millions of hungry people, just how important is it to be in style?

Jesus certainly understands our desire to have nice things. He knows it's difficult for us to go without items that everyone else seems to have. Furthermore, He never says that nice things are evil in and of themselves. Nevertheless, if we read the words Jesus said while He was on this earth, we soon realize that He was absolutely convinced that money could easily become an obstacle to the kingdom of His Father. And, today, we must admit that Jesus is much more concerned with our level of compassion than He is with our level of fashion. He would much rather have us impress others with our lives than with our possessions.

MOVING AHEAD

"We are living in a material world, and I am a material girl!" So sings one of today's hottest female rock stars. It's not difficult to see where she got her evidence. One young lawyer stated in a *Newsweek* interview—apparently without batting an eye—that she "would be comfortable with $200,000 a year." In the same article, a 29-year-old television executive proclaimed his desire was to have more money than he could possibly spend.[4] When we read about these people, we quickly say: "That's not me!" But have you ever asked yourself: Do I worship money? Do I spend it in the way God wants me to? Could I convince a Third World citizen that my spending habits are biblical?

Whether we make $25 a week mowing lawns or $2500

a week selling insurance, God is concerned with how we spend our money. Here are some things we can do that just might help us work our way through this challenging issue:

1. *Work on this issue in community*—In other words, discuss the problem of materialism with your Christian friends. Then try to come to some conclusions. Although you won't always agree, chances are that you will find some common ground. And then take action—together! Abandoning a stylish but expensive fashion may be too scary to do on your own. However, giving it up will undoubtedly be much easier if your friends are giving it up as well.

2. *Listen to people in less privileged economic circumstances*—Persons from the Third World often possess insights that we don't have. We often feel sorry for them because they are trapped in their poverty. But they sometimes feel sorry for us too, because they see us trapped in our affluence. A pastor from Latin America was once asked how his church survived in such a repressive system. His reply was startling. "Frankly," he said, "I feel the affluence of the Christians in North America is a more serious threat to the church in the United States than political repression is to our church."[5] Think about that for a minute!

3. *Begin where you are, one step at a time*—When we read Jesus' warnings about possessions, it is tempting to become discouraged. We read the parable of the rich ruler and conclude that our only option is all-or-nothing, and since we are not about to give up everything, we instead give up nothing. If you are discouraged by the all-or-nothing option, remind yourself that your Christian walk is just that—a walk. And regardless of where you might be on your walk, God simply requires that

you make His kingdom your top priority and seek after it, one step at a time. Your first step might be sponsoring a film on world hunger in order to educate your whole congregation, or it might be deciding as a youth group to give up a stylish but expensive fashion. But whatever it is, step out in faith. Your reward will be an abundance that money can't buy.

Notes

1. Arthur Simon, *Bread for the World* (New York: Paulist Press, 1984), p. 7.
2. *Ibid.*, p. 143.
3. Robert N. Bellah, *The Broken Covenant* (New York: Seabury Press, 1975), p. 133.
4. *Newsweek,* December 31, 1984.
5. Doris Janzen Longacre, *Living More with Less* (London: Hodder and Stoughton, 1982), p. 53.

4

Rock 'n' Roll
and the Arts

David Edwards

Orange, crackling flames dance high into the crisp evening air. Someone in the congregation shouts, "Praise
God!" The crowd answers with murmurs and mimic cries.

"These are the last to be burned," says the leader,
holding up the remaining articles of devilish fuel for everyone to see. "This vulgarity won't be poisoning *our* young
people anymore!" He tosses the offending articles into the
fire, lifts his hands toward heaven, and sighs, "Thank you
Jesus!" Then he leads the group in a hymn of thanksgiving.

A record-burning service somewhere in the midwest-
ern United States? In the late 1970s maybe, or the eight-
ies? No. The year is 1526, and the bonfire is being fueled,
not by rock music recordings, but by the first New Testa-

ments ever printed in the English language. Three thousand copies of the controversial books were printed the year before, by William Tyndale.[1] Only six copies now remain. All the rest were lost, or destroyed by the Church of England, which considered the very idea of an English Bible vulgar and blasphemous.[2]

"Oops!" the church would now say. It would say it, that is, if the "church" had the *collective* wherewithal to speak as one body. But she has never been quite the unified body of believers she was intended to be. So we use the term loosely when we talk about how the "church" has behaved at any given time. It's a lot like America. Not everyone in America was in favor of fighting the North Vietnamese. It may have been Lyndon Johnson who ordered such and such a bombing raid. But it was nevertheless America that fought in the war. And it may have been Henry VIII who ordered Tyndale's Bibles burned. But they were nevertheless burned, historically speaking, by the church. Only God Himself can use the term "true church" and know who He is talking about.

We're going to be talking about art and rock music and the church. These are touchy subjects. The church's bonfires have never gone out. She continues to exert an influence on world events, especially as regards the way we all express ourselves in art forms and other media.

We live in a world flooded with products of art. And though it now bombards us in unprecedented volume, the essential nature of that art has never changed. That is because human nature never changes. People go on saying the same kinds of things century after century. But whenever new art forms appear, the church often wants to get rid of them. This is supposedly better than putting up with their evil side, which corresponds to the worst side of human nature.

Nowadays, the most controversial art form is rock music, and the church is still divided about what to do with it. But we can't all wait for the church's decision about rock or any other art form. We are responsible for our own standards and our own decisions, whether we have the church's agreement or not. But to make those decisions, there are a few things we need to understand about the soul of art, or the particular element of human nature that happens to lie at the heart of a song or a painting or a play.

THE SOUL OF ART

All artists put their own personalities into their art. They cannot avoid doing so. Even if a songwriter *tries* to be dishonest, his song will convey insincerity to the discriminating listener. This is especially true when Christian songwriters try to *appear* religious. Their songs have a phoney ring to them, and sooner or later their true selves will be found out. So whether that songwriter is a heavenly or devilish person, the truth will be known.

This is not to say the best art is always heavenly, or the worst, devilish. Sometimes poor workmanship dresses a heavenly thought in shoddy attire; a moment's attention to almost any Christian radio station will provide several examples. On the other hand we often see the product of moral disease, clothed by genius, in the garments of artistic excellence. The brilliant but morally deranged Edgar Allen Poe is a good example. So is a rock group that makes great records but fails to say anything wholesome or positive in its lyrics. Good workmanship sometimes goes hand in hand with evil ideas.

But we are sailing into treacherous waters when we talk of workmanship. We cannot separate the physical body of a work of art from its soul the way we can separate the words of a song from the music accompanying it. If there is something wrong with the outward appearance of a painting, it may reflect some imperfection in the soul of the thing painted and in the soul of the artist. It may be something as simple as an embarrassing lack of discipline. By the same token, if that painting looks very good, it may indicate something about the painter that is good. So we may find something to admire in the sheer discipline or God-given talent behind the wonderfully crafted writings of troubled men like Poe or Hemingway. This is in spite of the fact that their work reflects decidedly non-Christian values.

CHRISTIAN AND NON-CHRISTIAN ARTISTS

We expect Christian artists, on the other hand, to reflect a Christ-like attitude. Their work ought to convey reverence, humility, and compassion, or even dismay with a culture that does not know Christian values. This of course is ideal, and it would be the rule if Christian artists weren't prone to corruption just like everyone else. But they are corruptible, and sometimes their work reflects hypocrisy, contempt, bigotry, and self-satisfaction; a gloating, pharisaical attitude.

The work of non-Christians runs the same gamut. A song written by a non-Christian may reflect a Christlike demeanor and yet espouse doctrinal beliefs (implied or expressed) that are unharmonious with Christianity. We may have ambivalent feelings about the song; there is something good or true or beautiful about it, and yet it also seems to be saying some things that are untrue. Or, if the song seems to plainly tell the truth, we may still respond with scepticism because the statement comes out of a belief system based on the wisdom of the world, which God says is folly. At the darkest end of the spectrum, the work of the non-Christian artist is hollow and spiritually impoverished; it is nothing but the despairing cry of a soul in torment and decay. Such is the case with much modern pop music. But Christians and non-Christians alike may convey the truth at some level.

TRUTH IN ART

The question of truth in art is tricky to address because there are so many levels of truth. At the lowest levels we have mere fact, like what time the sun will rise in the morning. This is easily conveyed, and is done so every day in the newspapers. But at the highest level are *Truths,* like God's omniscience, which at best are only partially comprehended and only imperfectly expressed.

It is not unusual for non-Christian artists to make statements in their art that are quite clearly true. There is nothing false in John Lennon's lyric, "All you need is love." In fact, it bears a striking resemblance to the apostle Paul's well-known treatise on love in 1 Corinthians 13. Shall we call Lennon's statement false because he is not a Christian? We'll be making nonsense if we do. Because the truth by any other name is still the truth. It doesn't suddenly become false as it leaves the mouth of someone we don't respect. A good way to describe Lennon's lyric is to call the truth of it incomplete. To say "All you need is love," without pointing to the source of love, is like telling the northern Africans all they need is water.

Here's another approach: Suppose our least favorite poet or essayist says, "Today it will rain somewhere in the world." Few will dispute the truth of this. Should we then say that the work of this artist conveys Truth? Not if we are using the word in its highest sense. Because again, a mere fact has been expressed, lying at the lowest levels of

Truth. If the artist says something about the divine *idea* of rain, his work rises to a higher level of Truth.

The highest Truth begins and ends in Christ. Jesus says, "I am the truth," and in saying so, He makes the idea of Truth more easily grasped than ever before. He makes the truth so concrete and visible, in fact, that many stumble over it. They cannot believe in a living, breathing embodiment of Truth. They can only deal in theories and abstractions.

As we take on more and more of the mind of Christ, our ability to see the truth or falseness in art increases because God judges the secrets of men and women through Jesus. And when we know Christ perfectly, we will have perfect discernment, recognizing all Truth in all forms of expression.

But is this practical for the average Christian? Yes. More than we realize. However little we know of the mind of Christ, it still affects every decision we make. Because even a speck of that knowledge triggers something in our conscience and changes the way we think and behave. So the answer to all questions of Truth in art is Christ Himself, the wisdom He gives us, and the obedience His goodness requires of us. Knowing *about* Him is abstract and useless. Knowing *the Man* is infinitely practical and has a good deal to do with the way we judge the potential effect of art.

ART AND MORALITY

And the effect we desire is a civilizing one. This is what society has always required of its artists. Art that seems to encourage immoral, violent, or antisocial behavior is, not surprisingly, looked upon unfavorably by society at large. This is in spite of the fact that in every age there are critics and patrons of the arts who seem to relish a bit of anarchy and debauchery.

Such was the case when Plato, writing more than three hundred years before Christ, warned his countrymen that their hedonistic life-styles would eventually bring disaster to the Greek civilization: "If you receive the pleasure-seasoned Muse, pleasure and pain will be kings in your city instead of law and agreed principles." Plato felt that too much of the drama and poetry of his day were providing mere entertainment, when they should have been providing direct stimulus to right thinking and right action.

While many of Plato's theological and aesthetic presuppositions were false or incomplete, much of what he said was remarkably accurate, especially his prediction that Greek civilization was due for imminent collapse.

Plato's words have a familiar ring in the twentieth century. Because today, artists and their patrons find themselves asking the same, ancient questions: "Is art a threat to society, or can it be helpful? It ought to have a high moral tone, but upon whose idea of morality should it be based? By whose standards shall we measure the value or harmfulness of a work of art?"

THE VOICE OF THE CHURCH

And the church is frequently in the thick of this controversy. In one age she exerts a positive influence on the arts, helping to shape progressive, worldwide trends. In another she proves herself a foe and persecutor of art. In all cases she purports to interpret Judeo-Christian thought and tradition. "Scripture," says the church, "is the standard for all questions of morality."

But the church has chronic amnesia; only isolated members of that worldwide body are aware of what her policies and practices have been over the centuries. This is partly because the church is fragmented into so many sects and denominations and partly because few of her members are interested in their history.

The church, therefore, is slow to learn from her mistakes. For example, the average churchgoer doesn't know the story about those early English New Testaments. And while Bible translation is more a science than an art, the church's treatment of William Tyndale (he was strangled and burned) illustrates an important point that has enormous bearing on the arts (and on the sciences). The church, throughout history, hasn't been keen on much of anything new. So when a new art form bears (or appears to bear) the first, inevitable fruit of corruption, she often hastily concludes that the form itself must be inherently evil.

This has been the case with everything from four-part harmony to motion pictures. But when enough time passes the church usually realizes she's dealing with an old problem; artists are putting into their art the same evil (or good) they always have. Artists are like all people. They have a universal tendency toward rebellion and corruption. When that tendency goes unchecked they make a hell for themselves, in which they love to wallow. Misery loves company. Disease loves to spread itself. It's all in a day's work of becoming like the devil. And if the evil candidate happens to be, say, a painter, his or her paintings will somehow reflect that misery and disease.

But woe to all the other painters (especially Christians) who just happen to use the same kind of media or technique as that devilish artist. Because now they must contend with the controversy their fellow painter has brought to an art form that, to them, is full of wholesome potential. Their beloved medium has now been tainted. And in the eyes of the church, it is highly suspect.

POP AND ROCK AS ART FORMS

Probably no art form the church has ever known has been more suspect than music. It comes full of power and brings division and controversy. It has sparked riots and revolutions, inspired armies, and subdued kings. And no music form has ever had a greater impact on the church than popular music. Popular music, once called *folk* music, includes all music suitable or intended for the people at large. (Nowadays the term *folk* is usually associated with one of the divisions of popular music.)

It doesn't take an expert to point to the most controversial of today's pop music. Most will agree it is rock. Since its inception in the 1950s, rock music has been associated with all the wrong company, the drug-pushing, fast-driving, rebellious, and morally loose juveniles from the wrong side of the tracks. Its detractors, who now span two generations, describe their enemy with the severest epithets: "Despicable, perverse, degenerate." And for a very good reason; the *culture* in which rock music often flourishes is sometimes more vile than they can imagine.

THE BABY AND THE BATHWATER

But every art form ever practiced has had its share of bad company, along with its share of abuse from the church. This, as we have said, is simply because art is made by humans. And their personalities run the whole gamut of spiritual experience, from saintliness to abject perversity. And in this one important respect, rock music is just like any other art form; it can be uplifting or degrading. At its worst, it makes the idea of wholesome rock music seem like an impossibility.

Such was the case with Wagner's music after Hitler popularized it at his Nazi war rallies during World War II. It was banned from Israel and wasn't publicly performed there till the 1980s, and only in spite of much public outcry.[3] The music itself had taken on the reputation of its wicked patrons. (The composer had contributed to this, decades earlier, with his own anti-Semitic statements.) What a shame if the Nazis were allowed to take not only the lives of innocent millions, but the musical heritage of the rest of the world!

But suppose they had. Suppose a treaty was signed calling for a worldwide ban on all German classical music and all German mythology of the Wagnerian type. Where would it end? Would all German music be banned? All German art? All Germans? Isn't that the best way to get rid of the whole Nazi plague?

Of course we know it is not. Most of us learned quite early in life the name of this kind of madness; it is called *throwing the baby out with the bathwater.* It is a mistake we have all made: Suzy broke my heart, so now I'll have nothing to do with Karen or Linda or Nancy; the neighbor's dog bit me, so now I distrust all dogs; I bought a faulty automobile from a Slobovian immigrant, and now I think everyone in his country is a crook. And here's one we've all heard: That TV preacher, The Reverend Roister Doister, is such a hypocritical, pompous jerk, that I refuse to take seriously anything having to do with Christianity.

Let's assume our particular baby is rock music. The bathwater is all the scum and trash, drugs and immorality that rock music could do without. But we can't throw out *all* rock 'n' roll. Some of it has many redeeming qualities, not the least of which is its ability to communicate Christian values to the people who are presently being poisoned by all that scum and trash.

We need to throw out all the scum, while saving the baby. And this is for reasons just as important as that of keeping what is salvageable. For if we once throw the baby out, we've established a precedent; *We don't know how to be selective in what we discard.*

So, we're likely to lose the next baby that comes along, which may be classical music. As we have seen, it may be found in the company of things like Wagnerian anti-Semitism (also just about every other sort of immorality you can name). Or, the next baby may be gospel music, which also comes with undesirable by-products, like false piety and greed and celebrity-worship. We've got to learn to distinguish between the baby and the bathwater, between operas and Nazis, between true religion and hypocrisy, between wholesome rock 'n' roll and poisonous rock 'n' roll.

THE DISCERNMENT FILTER

What we need is some kind of filter that allows us to discard the bathwater while saving the baby. This filter is *discernment.* The dictionary defines discernment as *the ability to distinguish, or separate out.* By this process, every product of art I see or hear passes through a filtering system that is used daily and is constantly being revised. It is no different from the filters that wiser Christians have been using for centuries.

The building blocks of discernment are knowledge and experience. They help us recognize the true nature of a thing. And once we see the truth, commitment is the glue that helps us stick to what we know is right. It helps us act according to our knowledge.

We all have discernment to some extent. When it is founded on wisdom it is supremely useful; it protects us from all that is unwholesome in an art form. But when that filter is clogged with ignorant presumption it "filters" out all sorts of things that God intended for us to enjoy. Like tomatoes. Can you bite into a plump, vine-ripened tomato and imagine that just a few hundred years ago these delectable things were considered poisonous? It was a matter of ignorant presumption.

And what happens when we have plenty of energetic commitment but not enough knowledge and experience? Then we have fanaticism. Fanaticism is excessive zeal or enthusiasm. It's like rocket fuel in a Volkswagen; instead of taking the car nearer its destination, it turns it into smouldering rubble. It is misguided energy.

HEAD-BANGING

It is fanatical to ban all of Wagner's music or all rock music or all of any kind of art form. It is fanatical because it expends the energy of commitment in a reckless way. Some call this *head-banging*. And since it takes such extraordinary determination to bang one's head for very long, some people admire the stamina and persistence of head-bangers.

We may categorize as head-banging any tactic that expends frustrated energy by recklessly bashing at anything—from an art form to the windows of a university. The fanatic must find some kind of target—best known as a scapegoat—simply because there is something wrong somewhere. And lashing out at even an innocent victim seems better than doing nothing. Aren't we glad few policemen act this way? Wouldn't it be unpleasant if a policeman said, "I know I should be shooting at someone over there; so rather than do nothing I'll just shoot at anyone in that general direction?"

APATHY

The opposite of head-banging is apathy. Apathy says, "I suppose there's nothing we can do. We'll just have to live with poisoned bathwater. We certainly can't throw the baby out." When it comes to rock 'n' roll, apathy might sound like this: "I can't research the philosophies and life-styles of every rock group I listen to. The words to rock songs probably don't mean anything anyway. What do you want me to do? Burn all my records?" The result of apathy is not much different from that of fanaticism. Because the poisoned bathwater is left just as it is, free to pursue its destructive course.

CUTTING OFF WHAT OFFENDS US

And is Jesus fanatical when He says, "If your eye causes you to sin, gouge it out and throw it away. It is better for you to enter life with one eye than to have two eyes and be thrown into the fire of hell" (Matt. 18:9). No, He is not. He takes a firm stance against apathy and fanaticism.

And any doctor can tell you why. Removing one part of the body in order to save the patient is something doctors do every day. It is not fanatical, but it is *drastic*. And at the other extreme is the pure, apathetic stupidity of ignoring the problem altogether.

We may apply Jesus' injunction in many ways, depending on what is likely to make each of us stumble. Some ought to cancel an MTV subscription (you can count me in). Others ought to avoid the records and concerts of certain rock groups. Obedience here is a willingness to forgo something that is harmless to some, but causes us to stumble because of some weakness in ourselves.

This may include entire art forms that are harmless to

one person and deadly to another. That's why some need to burn their records and others don't. Discarding a collection of records is not throwing the baby out; those particular records may be the epitome of foul bathwater.

But if we find it necessary to take such drastic steps on our own behalf, let's avoid a common mistake: Some have assumed that because their eye needed plucking out, it followed that their God-given duty was to pluck out the eyes of everyone else.

YES TO THE BEST, NO TO THE WORST

Well-intentioned fanaticism throws the baby down the drain. Unintentional apathy forfeits it. Is this a dilemma? It often seems so. But it's really more like a balancing act. We have to strike a balance between apathy and fanaticism. Because whether we like it or not, we are responsible for the decisions we make.

We are created in the image of the Creator. Our ability to make and enjoy art is part of the divine idea of what we were intended to be. If every art form that ever conveyed an evil thought were erased from the memory of mankind, we would be left with no music, no literature, no painting, no sculpture. Not one art form would be left.

When God offers the gift of creativity we can say, "No thanks. I might expose myself to something harmful." This is fanaticism. Through the years it has been the distinguishing mark of dozens of Christian sects. One group in nineteenth century Scotland called for a ban on all fiddle music. Another shunned anything recorded on celluloid film. And in the last half of the twentieth century we find certain factions in the church trying to convince us that syncopation will call up demons.

All these fanatical positions are wrong because they

reject the fact that "every good and perfect gift is from above" (Jas. 1:17). They fail to realize that everything in God's creation is perfect until someone gets hold of part of it and temporarily spoils it. They fail to realize that any art form ever corrupted by humans can be redeemed by God.

At the opposite of fanaticism, we lazily say yes when we ought to say no; we are gullible when someone offers a contaminated version of one of God's gifts. Our responsibility is to say yes to the best and no to the garbage, while allowing others the same freedom to make their own choices.

Art at its best is one of the noblest, loftiest accomplishments of humankind. The work of a Bach or a Michelangelo inspires, uplifts, enriches the world. But at its worst, art is a poison; its effect is degrading and pernicious. And sometimes that poison is not easy to detect. But God doesn't expect us to throw up our hands and say, "This is too much trouble. I can't deal with it." He expects us to live the lives He has given us, using the wisdom and discernment He promises to provide, picking out the good from the bad, enjoying His perfect gifts until the day when all stumbling blocks are removed and nothing remains but the pure and the holy and the undefiled.

Notes

1. *Webster's Biographical Dictionary* (Springfield, MA: G. and C. Merriam Company, 1970), p. 1497.

2. John Wycliffe made an English translation of the Bible in 1382, before Gutenberg's printing press was developed. It was no more popular with church leaders than Tyndale's would be.

3. Moshe Brilliant, in *The New York Times,* Saturday, October 17, 1981, reported on an October 16 concert in the Mann Auditorium, Tel Aviv, in which the Israel Philharmonic performed the Prelude and "Liebestod" from Richard Wagner's *Tristan und Isolde.* The article described how several concertgoers became violent over the Wagner performance, coming to blows with security personnel in the auditorium. Brilliant wrote on Tuesday, October 20, that Wagner's music had been boycotted in Israel since World War II, because the nineteenth-century German composer was an anti-Semite and his music an inspiration for the Nazis.

5

Everybody Isn't Doing It!

Jim Burns

You've heard the same statistics I've heard when it comes to high schoolers engaging in sexual intercourse. At least 50 percent of all high school students will have had sexual intercourse by the time they are 18 years old. These statistics are staggering. Each year there are over one million high school women in America who become unwed mothers. In one year alone over four hundred thousand girls between 15 and 18 will make the decision to have an abortion. When you read the statistics and hear the news about high school sexuality you can get depressed and for a good reason. There are millions of students hurting their lives because they aren't handling their sexuality in a positive manner.

However, what about the 50 percent of high schoolers who are choosing not to have sexual intercourse? There are millions of high school students who are dealing with their sexuality in a different way. They've chosen to wait. Do they have the same curiosity and temptations? Yes. Have they wondered "What would it be like to have sexual intercourse?" Of course. Has their fantasy life been as active as others? Most likely. There are no easy answers as to why some people choose to have sexual intercourse before marriage and others wait. Yet I firmly believe that those who have waited and overcome their sexual temptations are today a happier, more fulfilled group of people.

Everyday, normal, red-blooded high school people choose to wait when it comes to "going all the way." Some of the people are like Robert who said, "I counted the cost and the cost was too high even though my feelings and emotions told me otherwise."

Julie's story was similar. "I thought at first guys wouldn't like me because I wouldn't have sex with them. I've never had a boy lose interest when he finds out I'm saving my virginity for my marriage partner."

Cindy's situation is a little different but just as important. "When I was in ninth grade I had sexual intercourse with a twelfth grader. I thought I was in love and let my emotions get carried away and before I knew it we were 'making love.' I must admit the feeling of closeness was not all bad but I kept thinking *this isn't what I really want.* We broke up two weeks later. I sort of felt empty. A year later I asked Jesus Christ to come into my life. He promised to forgive my sins and my relationship with Tom was first on the list of sins that needed to be forgiven in my mind. Not only has God forgiven me, He is helping me not to settle for second best in relationships. By His strength I'm developing a meaningful relationship with a Christian guy and although we could easily be tempted God is helping us."

These are but a few of the stories of young men and women who live exciting, fulfilled lives and have chosen to refrain from sexual intercourse in premarital relationships. The fact is: Everybody isn't doing it!

WHY WAIT?

For the Christian, having sex before marriage is a sin. The Bible is explicit when it says in the Ten Commandments, "You shall not commit adultery" Exod. 20:14). In the New Testament we are also challenged to refrain from sexual intercourse before marriage. "It is God's will that you should be holy; that you should avoid sexual immorality" (1 Thess. 4:3).

When Christians have intercourse before marriage it doesn't mean that they are no longer Christians; it does mean they are "missing the mark" in being all that God desires them to be. Christians have the same sexual temptations as people who have not chosen Jesus Christ to be Lord of their lives. Yet the difference for the Christian is that having sexual intercourse before marriage is a known sin and sin keeps us from living out the will of God in our lives. More and more I'm meeting Christians like those mentioned at the beginning of this chapter who are choosing to go against the grain of our culture. People who are not buying into the philosophy of many today who say, "If it feels good do it." Young men and women are developing positive relationships with those of the opposite sex and choosing to save sexual intercourse for marriage.

Is there an easy answer to overcoming sexual temptation? No. A magic formula or a secret solution? Absolutely not! However, there are some practical guidelines that if taken seriously will help you avoid settling for second best when it comes to your sex life.

GUIDELINES FOR OVERCOMING SEXUAL TEMPTATION

As we begin looking at these guidelines let me remind you that the Christian faith is a radical faith. Sometimes it goes against the grain of our culture. Sometimes to be a follower of Jesus Christ means to take an unpopular stand or to refuse to settle for mediocrity when it seems that the entire world is going in a different direction. These guidelines are for those who desire to grow in their faith and for those who desire to let God be a part of their relationship with the opposite sex.

Radical Respect

Our culture has taught us to look at people of the opposite sex as sex objects. The amount of sexual teasing that goes on even at Christian events always amazes me. The Bible calls men and women to a relationship that I call one of radical respect. Look at Paul's advice on how to treat others: "Do nothing out of selfish ambition or vain conceit, but in humility consider others better than yourselves. Each of you should look not only to your own interests, but also to the interests of others" (Phil. 2:3).

The way I look at it, Christians are challenged to treat each other as "miniature Jesus Christs." What I mean is that since we are all created in the image of God and Jesus dwells inside each and every believer, we are to respect the Jesus living inside one another. This concept can change the way we view our dating life and sex habits. That Christian guy or girl you are dating is no longer a person to experiment with sexually. He or she is a Christian brother or sister and you are called by God to "look to the interests of others." I would go so far to say we should treat every person on a date the way we would want someone to be treating our future husband or wife.

As you can understand, this issue of radical respect can be far-reaching and life-changing. It really does take a lot of work to begin treating others as children of God. But no one ever said doing it the right way would necessarily be the easiest way. So go ahead: Go against the grain of culture and learn to respect others with a supernatural radical respect.

Setting Standards

Emotional involvement that exceeds a person's level of maturity can lead to the wrong sexual decisions.

Let's face it, sexual attraction and romance are fun and very real in the life of every normal human being. There are times when even the strongest individuals get carried away in the emotion of the moment and sexual temptation becomes a reality. This is why people who choose to refrain from sexual intercourse before marriage must learn to set standards.

Perhaps you've heard the phrase, "He or she who aims at nothing gets there every time." This phrase applies to sexual temptation as well. If you set standards not when you are at Inspiration Point but rather in your home with a clear head you could save yourself from great disappointment.

The best advice Cathy and I received before our marriage was from our minister. He challenged us to set standards. He asked us to discuss over a Coke at McDonald's where our sexual standards would best glorify God and where we felt comfortable setting our standards before marriage. We did just that. Then in the heat of emotion we knew that if we began to violate the standards we had set we were going against some basic principles of our relationship.

My suggestion is that on your own sometime soon, you think through the whole aspect of petting. In other words, how far is too far for you? Many a person has experienced a great amount of heartbreak and emptiness because he or she never took this simple step of setting standards.

The other advice I would give before moving to the next point is that if you are involved in a relationship today where you are too physically involved, then talk with your boyfriend or girlfriend today about setting standards. If he or she will not cooperate, you need to question the validity of your relationship. If you do set standards and continually fall short of those standards maybe it's time to take a long, serious look at your relationship. What is your relationship based on? Is your relationship one of radical respect?

Dating: A Different Approach

I'm totally for dating. Although a date can be frightening or boring, most of the time dating is one of the high points of life. There are people who date early in life and others don't date until they are in college or even out of college.[1] No matter when you date, there are some important points to ponder about your dating life that can literally make the difference in your future happiness.

All dates do not have to be romantic. The great American date of dinner, movie, and make-out is not all it is cracked up to be. We date for the purpose of getting to know someone, enjoying each other's company, figuring out what type of person we would like to marry and actually practicing at working on relationships with the opposite sex. Although romance is enjoyable it is only a very small purpose of a date at the beginning of a relationship. The movie and make-out part of the great American date leaves little room for getting to talk to the person of the opposite sex.

My suggestion is to be creative with your dates and look at dating not from the cultural view that we see in the media. For example, what's wrong with two girls taking one guy kite flying at the local lake and then having a picnic dinner? Is that a date? Certainly it is a date—but just a different kind of date than what our culture calls a date. Can you have as much fun on "group dates" as on a single date? Sometimes you can have more fun. (Though this doesn't mean I'm against one-on-one dating.) If we let our imaginations work dating can be much more fun and enjoyable. I remember when a group of five girls and four guys went horseback riding, ate pizza at the beach and stayed up and talked in our college dorm until 2:00 in the morning. Would you call this a date? I would. In fact, I ended up marrying one of the five girls.

Tom and Carol started dating when Carol was 15. They had been boyfriend and girlfriend since eighth grade and finally began to date "officially" the night Tom turned 16. They dated all through tenth, eleventh, and half of twelfth grade and then they broke up. Yes, they were involved sexually. In fact that ended up being one of the reasons for the breakup. After their breakup they both told me at different times that they felt friendless. Both of them told me that they had put so much time and energy into this one high school romance that they really had never pursued other relationships with those of the same sex or the opposite sex. They were both lonely and hurting. Even though they knew their relationship was through, out of their loneliness they tried again. Of course it didn't work and only made matters more complicated.

I tell you this story only to say: *Caution. Exclusive dating can be hazardous to your life when you are in high school.* Now I don't mean you should never exclusively date somebody. That would be a ridiculous suggestion. However, the Tom and Carol story is played over and over again on every high school campus in America. If you don't want to become like Tom and Carol, pursue other outside friendships. If you have an exclusive dating relationship that is basically centered around sex don't wait to do something about it. The longer you wait the harder it is to make the right decisions.

One more thought about dating. *The people you choose to date will influence the way you carry out your Christian commitment.* This thought may be unpopular with some high school students, but I believe it to be the truth. It's my opinion that if you choose to date people who do not have a faith in Jesus Christ you are playing with fire when it comes to your Christian commitment. I'm not saying that all non-Christians are evil and you shouldn't associate with them. I'm not saying that every person who has ever dated a non-Christian is a sinner. I am saying that in my opinion many people who date persons with no Christian commitment end up watering down their faith and compromising their values. If Jesus Christ is the number one element in your life and He is not a part of your boyfriend or girlfriend's life then how can you be as close as two Christians? This is where I leave it to your "heart of hearts." Most people know what is right. They know if a relationship is strengthening their faith or hurting their faith. I stick with the statement: The people you choose to date will be a decisive factor in how you carry out your Christian commitment.

Your Body . . . God's Temple

Listen to what the apostle Paul said about your body. "Flee from sexual immorality. All other sins a man commits are outside his body, but he who sins sexually sins against his own body. Do you not know that your body is a temple of the Holy Spirit, who is in you, whom you have received from God? You are not your own; you were bought at a price. Therefore honor God with your body" (1 Cor. 6:18-20).

I think one of the reasons God states so clearly in Scripture that we should refrain from intercourse until marriage is that He dwells in our bodies. Our bodies are literally temples of God's Holy Spirit, and we are called to glorify God the best we can with our bodies.

Some people say, "God is the great killjoy when it comes to sex." No, He created sex and sees it as beautiful. In fact, the way I read Scripture He sees His creation of sexuality as a gift to us and sacred. Because He sees sex as such a special sacred gift He wants the best for us and that is why He challenges us to refrain until marriage.

It Comes Down to a Matter of Choice

Everybody isn't doing it! People choose to have sex or not have sex before marriage.[2] It comes down to a matter of choice, your choice. Our sexuality is an important part of our lives and our Christian faith. How you deal with your sexuality will greatly affect many of the other parts of your life. Sex can have an effect on your self-esteem, belief in God, friendships, personality and general behavior. Don't take the subject lightly. Learn all you can about your sexuality. After all, your sex life is God's special gift to you.

If You've Already Experienced Sex

Maybe you have already had sexual intercourse and

are wondering if you have forever lost your opportunity to have a close relationship with God. Don't despair. The Lord is always ready to forgive those who seek His cleansing (see 1 John 1:9). Forgiveness is part of the package of love and reconciliation that Jesus' death and resurrection made possible (see Rom. 5:6-11).

Epilogue

Some people would view me as rather prudish. Yet I really don't think I am. I've worked with so many people who hurt and hurt badly because of lousy sex lives. These are not dirty, rotten, evil people. They are young men and women who are a lot like you and me. People who truly desire to be God's people and yet because of our human nature fall short of God's best. I urge you to allow God to be a part of your dating life from the very first. He wants the best for you. Some people have the impression that if they give their dating life to God He'll turn them into hermits. This simply isn't true. God created male and female and He wants them to have a good, positive, healthy relationship. Don't forget that He created sex. I figure since He created sex He is the only one who has the right to tell us what is best for us when it comes to sexuality. Don't be afraid to seek His help. Remember: Everybody isn't doing it!

Notes

1. Some authorities have said that up to 50 percent of all American girls have never been on a date when they graduate. If you fall into this category you are definitely not alone!

2. I am not overlooking the tragedy of rape or incest. If either has happened or is happening in your life do not wait another moment to seek help. There is hope. There is help. There are people who understand your problem. Do not hesitate to talk with them today.

6

Homosexuality

Don Williams

There was a time in our culture when nobody would talk about homosexuality (sexual attraction for persons of the same sex). Then the lid blew off this subject. Gay or homosexual people went into the streets preaching "Gay is good." They identified themselves with liberation movements such as black liberation and women's liberation. They demanded full civil rights. They demanded full acceptance by the church. They claimed, "God has made us this way. My being gay is not a deviation from God's good creation but a variation of that creation made by Him."

Christians need to deal with the issue of homosexuality for several reasons. First, about 5 percent of the adult males and 2 percent of the adult females in our country identify themselves as homosexual. Thus, there are numbers of gay people in our schools, churches, and communities. Whether we know it or not we are relating to them.

Second, many gays are advocating a "gay life-style" and claiming that there is no moral, psychological, or spiritual problem with being gay. Even the American Psychiatric Association no longer sees homosexuality as a problem of emotional illness.

Third, many younger people are struggling with homosexual feelings. "What does this mean?" they ask; "Am I gay?"

Fourth, some Christians who are also homosexual claim that the Bible is not opposed to homosexuality as such and that all that really matters to God are healthy, monogamous, committed sexual relationships, whether straight or gay. This final point leads us to the heart of this chapter—what does the Bible really say about homosexuality? How are we to understand this human condition from God's point of view?

WHERE DO WE BEGIN?

The first issue we must face when turning to God's Word is: Where should we begin to read? Those who advocate that Christians who are practicing homosexuals should be fully accepted in the church *as they are* begin their reading with the story of Sodom and Gomorrah in Genesis 19:1-29. They point out that this story refers to God's judgment upon Sodom for homosexual rape. Next, they rightly say that all gay Christians are also opposed to homosexual rape, just as heterosexual Christians are.

Then they turn to the laws against male homosexual acts in Leviticus 18:22 and 20:13. Here they claim that these laws refer to male cult prostitutes and are there because of the idolatry involved in the cultic act. Furthermore, they claim that these laws are equal to other laws in Leviticus such as those against making cloth out of two kinds of thread (like cotton and wool). Thus if we enforce the laws against homosexual acts why don't we enforce the laws against mixing nylon and rayon?

Turning to the New Testament, gay advocates point out that Jesus said nothing about homosexuality. If He was silent (it is supposed) He must not have cared about the subject. It is Paul, of course, who talks a lot about homosexuality (see Rom. 1:26,27; 1 Cor. 6:9; 1 Tim. 1:9,10). Homosexual Christians who advocate their gay life-style claim that Paul only knew about "perverts" (heterosexual people who commit homosexual acts) rather than "inverts" (people who never knew a time when they were not attracted sexually to the same sex). Thus, they claim, Paul has nothing to say to most homosexual people who have not chosen their homosexual orientation, but who have always felt their same-sex attraction.

Is it proper, however, to read the Bible in such a proof-texting way? Should we just look up all the individual references to homosexuality and then try to draw our conclusions? If we don't do this, what should our approach be?

BEGIN WITH GENESIS

Simply speaking, the alternative is to start reading the Bible at the beginning, namely in Genesis 1. The advantage of this is that the texts on homosexuality will then be placed in the context of the whole of the Word of God. Jesus Himself follows this method when He argues against divorce by going back to creation, what God intended when He made us male and female and ordained the permanent bond of marriage (see Matt. 19:3-9).

If we start then by reading Genesis 1—2 what do we discover about the creation of human beings and their sexual relationship as God ordained them? Read these chapters and then consider the following points:

1. God made us in His image as male and female. He shows that His character is fully reflected only in a heterosexual community. God is not fully seen in a male-male community or in a female-female community.

2. God blessed heterosexual sexual union and saw as the outcome the procreation of the race. Thus, biologically our genital structure is made for heterosexual union.

3. When it was not good for man to be alone God did not create a second man, but a woman. Same-sex relationships cannot assuage our created loneliness.

4. God's purpose in creation was that Adam and Eve be united in the monogamous, permanent, heterosexual sexual union of "one flesh." This is impossible in same-sex relationships.

When we keep on reading in Genesis 3 we discover that the goodness of creation has been ruined by the Fall. It was the seduction of Satan (as the serpent) and the entrance of sin which perverted God's original intention for our sexuality. Thus, we must conclude that homosexuality is not a result of God's good creation (see Gen. 1-2) but a result of its disruption in the Fall (see Gen. 3).

If this is true, then it is no surprise that in Sodom (see Gen. 19) homosexual rape is a sin. Moreover, it is a sin for two reasons. First, forced sexual relations with anyone is a violent violation of the person. Second, same-sex relations violate God's order in creation where He made us for heterosexual union.

Now we can also understand why the laws in Leviticus 18:22 and 20:13 prohibit male sexual acts with males. They do so not because of the sin of cult prostitution (it is hard to see how homosexual acts can be related to the fertility cults around Israel) but because of the sin of corrupting God's order for our sexuality being expressed in a heterosexual union. Moreover, these laws are enduring because they express God's order in creation and are reaffirmed in the New Testament. This is not true, however, of the laws about mixing threads.

Here someone might ask, "But what about the law that those who engage in homosexual acts should be put to death (see Lev. 20:13)? Certainly you don't believe that this law should be enforced." The answer is, "Yes, those who do this should be put to death, along with murderers, adulterers, liars, and racists." All sin deserves death (see Ezek. 18:4; Rom. 6:23). The good news, however, is that Christ has been put to death in place of us poor sinners. He has died for homosexual persons and heterosexual persons; straights and gays.

LIGHT FROM THE NEW TESTAMENT

Well, then, if the Old Testament is clear that homosexual acts are sin, why is Jesus silent on the subject? There are two answers to this question. In the first place, Jesus didn't address homosexuality because it was not an issue among the Jews. They experienced little or no homosexuality. It was only in the Greco-Roman world that homosexuality was practiced. Therefore, it was Paul who had to deal with it, not Jesus.

In the second place, whenever Jesus did speak about human sexuality He always presupposed heterosexuality (compare Matt. 5:27,28). Thus, as we have mentioned, when Jesus voiced His opposition to divorce He went back to Creation for the basis of His argument and ruled out divorce because "it was not this way from the beginning" (Matt. 19:8). If Jesus had had to address homosexuality He certainly would have made a similar argument.

When we turn to Paul then we find the most specific verses on homosexuality in the whole Bible. In Romans 1:26,27 Paul speaks of lesbians (female homosexuals) as well as male homosexuals. The objection of gay advocates that Paul knew nothing of "inverts," those who have always been attracted to the same sex, contains an element of truth. Paul viewed all homosexual acts as a perversion of human sexual relations. He did so, not because he was ignorant of modern psychological data, but because of Genesis 1—2. Because God created us for heterosexual relationships, all homosexual acts, be they by "perverts" or "inverts," are sinful and a sign, as stated in Romans 1, of the wrath of God turning us over to our sin, and the loss of human identity and the brokenness of human relationships in this world.

CONCLUSIONS

What then can we conclude from this study of homosexuality from the Bible?

1. Homosexuality is not a part of God's good creation but a result of the Fall and sin's entrance into the world. It therefore disrupts God's original order for the sexes.

2. Homosexual desire should be viewed as a sickness like cancer or heart disease. Same-sex desire, although not consciously chosen by a gay person, is a corruption of the sexual desire which is created to be directed toward the opposite sex.

3. Homosexual desire (temptation) becomes sin when

it is nurtured and acted upon (compare Jas. 1:13-15).

4. When homosexual desire is not acted upon it is still a distortion of God's good creation and is guilt-provoking and damaging. Thus, this desire should be healed and gays should be released from homosexual bondage. Judith Mac-Nutt, a psychotherapist, has had a 100 percent cure rate for homosexual persons through a combination of professional counseling and prayer-therapy for inner healing (the healing of past hurts and emotional damage).

5. Homosexual persons come to Christ just as heterosexual persons do—by repenting of their sins and accepting Jesus as their Saviour and Lord. As Christians, homosexual persons then need the healing of God in the community of the church. There can be no place in the church for the rejection of gays as *persons*. But we cannot accept their homosexual orientation as God's best for them.

6. Teenagers who have homosexual feelings need to know that this does not necessarily mean that they are "gay." In fact, God creates all of us "straight." Such feelings and fantasies may come and go on the route to sexual maturity. If some teens are troubled by these feelings a professional Christian counselor can be of great help.

In the New Testament Paul speaks of sinners who now make up the church. Included in the list are homosexual persons. He then goes on to say, "But you were washed, you were sanctified, you were justified in the name of the Lord Jesus Christ and by the Spirit of our God" (1 Cor. 6:11). There is hope for the homosexual person in Christ. This is good news in our broken world!

7

Bigotry

John M. Perkins

I want to look at how I have been affected by bigots, as well as some effects I have observed with the hatred and behavior of biased persons. First let me define the term bigot as I see it. A bigot is a person who has an unreasonable and blind hatred towards any other person who holds an opinion or is of a race or creed that differs from his or her own. A bigot believes that he or she knows what another person or race of people ought to have, to be, or to do. A bigot will not only hate, but will turn that hatred into a certain amount of pain which can only be released when it is directed personally against those people who are hated. It seems that the situation is relieved and the bigot is affirmed if there is a strong group, race, or class that agrees with the bigot's opinion or at least will follow his or her action against the biased group. So a bigot then is one who is full of internal hatred and pain, but thinks that the pain is released when it is directed toward others, and whose drive and motivation are directed toward the ease of the pain. Bigotry is the compounded form of prejudice.

BIGOTRY IN THE BIBLE

One of the clearest biblical examples of bigotry is found in Acts chapter 12 in the actions of King Herod. Here we see a sudden, violent eruption of hostility towards the Christians with seemingly no cause except that Peter was now accepting Gentiles into the Jewish-Christian church. This new command from God began to stir up a lot of trouble even among church members themselves. But the bigoted non-Christian community was even more alarmed. Remember, the Jews hated the Gentiles. As long as the early church was almost entirely Jewish, the Jewish authorities would let it exist in peace, for the most part, with only an occasional expression of hostility.

But when it became obvious that the church was accepting Gentiles into its ranks, this was too much for both the Jewish population as a whole and the Jewish authorities. So in Acts chapter 12 King Herod decided to make a show of his power by executing James, the apostle (see v. 2). This was just a test case, a trial balloon. If the people objected, he would allow the whole matter to simmer down. But because the people were pleased (see v. 3), Herod went on to put Peter in jail, planning to execute him later.

Here we see that Herod's hatred for the Gentiles turned into pain which he wanted to release against the

Gentiles. When the other Jewish people supported his efforts, he increased those efforts. The remainder of the chapter tells how God interfered with this plan by sending an angel to deliver Peter from that prison. And even today God is looking for His people to stand up and allow themselves to be used as instruments of His righteousness and justice.

God's heart has not changed; His Word is clear to state that "God does not show favoritism" (Rom. 2:11).

Now let me share some examples of bigotry that I have experienced in my own life. I want to look at some of the effects that these experiences have had in my development and even possibly share my response to some of these situations.

"WHO ARE YOU THE DADDY OF?"

The earliest memory of such an experience was when I was a little boy five or six years old in our little town of New Hebron, Mississippi. Now my mother had died when I was seven months old and I was raised by my grandmother who lived in a little sharecroppers' shack a mile or two outside of town. Now there were no black people who lived within the city limits of New Hebron except the cooks who lived in the back of the white people's homes. All the other blacks would have to live outside the town limits, so going into town was always something to look forward to as little boys. We would usually end up talking with some of the white boys and interacting with them.

On one of my first visits I remember this one white boy coming up to my cousin Jimmy and me, and he wanted to ask us a question. He asked me, "Who are you the daddy of?" And as a five- or six-year-old boy, I answered him by saying that I was the daddy of Jap Perkins, who was my father. Jap did not live with us but I knew that he was my daddy. When I gave this answer I remember how the white boys just laughed and laughed at me. I had thought they were asking me whose son I was and it took me a long time before I understood that joke and why they laughed so hard at me. I think at that early age, the white boys had been taught and told that we black boys were ignorant and inferior. And my not knowing that I did not have a son reinforced that bias to them.

I can clearly remember this very incident and I guess that began to formulate in my own life some opinions that caused me to hate inside. Realizing that someone was trying to make me feel inferior, and being uncertain about anybody loving me anyway, affected my opinions about myself and my race. Even at that point, I felt that society had made us to believe that white folks were better than us because the materialism they had around them was better. In our town of New Hebron, usually what people possessed was the basis for good and bad, and the bigoted southern white culture was dictating that philosophy without it being questioned.

Another incident from my childhood happened at the bus station in Columbia when I went to visit my father. Now this was a great event to travel 50 miles away from home. I was expecting and anticipating this trip for a long time and I felt really special to get to go. This was my first time in a bus station, and I think my dad left me there briefly while he went outside to speak with some of his friends. But I remember in that bus station there were all of these black people in this dark back room, and I could look over through the window where I saw all of these white people in this nice place. But I remember that there was an old lady there and I remember watching as she went out of our room to the other side to get a ticket or at least information from the ticket agent. The lady was nervous and afraid that she was not going to get the ticket that she needed, and she interfered with the agent while he was talking with another white person. This interruption caused the agent to turn around and we all watched as he cursed this old lady and threatened her like he was going to come over and beat her up, and in fact said so. I was a little boy, and I looked around in that room expecting those men in that room to get up and to fight this man for talking to this old black lady the way he talked to her. But as I looked around in the room, I saw those old men sitting quiet, some beginning to leave the room, and no one daring to confront him.

That made an impression on me, how that we as blacks were being so processed by bigots who had inward hatred. This man acted like he was mad and his search for his own affirmation caused him to release his pain toward other people. He wanted that room full of people to know who was boss, yet his hatred grew and could not be satisfied.

Even as a child I watched this behavior as I grew up in the south. I could always see the young white people wanting us to call them "Mister" when we would meet on the street. If we were ever stopped by a highway patrol or sheriff, they would shape their words in a way that you had to say "Yes Sir," or "Mister," and most of the blacks learned how to live in that system. When we would see a white person coming, we would walk out the door and begin to say, "Yes Sir, Boss," or "Yes Sir, Mister," to affirm them. I would watch as many of those bigots then would turn around and really believe that they were loved by those black people who were simply trying to survive and get by in that system. We were supposed to make the white man happy, we were supposed to be "sambos," "jamup and honey," "step and fetch it." Not only were we to make the white man happy but we ourselves were supposed to be happy. And this constant struggle was what made the civil rights movement break out in the sixties.

It happened again when I was 12 years old. I remember seeing a white man from a nearby plantation busy hauling hay. The man was in a hurry to get that hay inside quickly before it rained. The man needed somebody to help him haul hay and I needed some money. So I took that opportunity to earn what I hoped would be $1.50 or $2.00. At least that was what they were paying for a day's work, and that's what I expected to get. I was thinking how great it would be to buy a new shirt or belt, or even a pocket-knife to take home and show the other kids. So I went to work and worked hard all day.

In the evening I went to the white gentleman's house to receive my pay and all I got was a dime and a buffalo nickel—just 15 cents. I had earned it, but at that point of anger and disappointment I didn't even know whether to take the money or not. Here was a white man handing it to me, I was in his house, I had worked for him, but I was afraid. Afraid if I accepted the money that I would hate myself because I knew my labor was worth more. Afraid too if I didn't take the money, the man would say I was an "uppity nigger" or maybe a "smart nigger." And at that time in Mississippi, being black was bad enough, but a smart nigger was even worse.

So here I was all alone, my first time going out on my own in the workaday world; my first confrontation with a white employer; and my first face-to-face encounter with "the system." But I couldn't do anything about it . . . so I took that 15 cents. But I went away from there asking all kinds of questions. What had happened? How could that white man take advantage of me like that? My opinions and hatred were reinforced.

SATURDAY NIGHT IN TOWN

Then when I was 16 years old something happened that I will never forget. Daily life in Mississippi at that time was hard, but every Saturday evening all the farm hands would come up from the fields at noon, stop working for the day, clean up and head to town to visit, shop, or just look around. Town was the real center of life. Town was also where the blacks and whites mixed, and where the real hatred, bigotry, and evil of the system came out. Of course the white man was boss and his system of law and order was simply to keep the blacks in line.

On this particular Saturday night, my older brother Clyde was taking his girlfriend Elma to the movies. Clyde was the hero to all of us younger kids. Clyde was like a second father, he had just gotten discharged from the army and we all looked up to him. But Clyde and Elma were standing in the alley, next to Carolyn's Theater, talking until the ticket booth would open. Nobody's real sure just what started it, but some folks think Clyde was kinda talking loud, maybe having an argument with Elma, when a deputy marshal standing on the sidewalk yelled at them, "You niggers quiet down." As Clyde turned to ask the marshal a question, the deputy clubbed him with his night stick. Clyde got mad and in self-defense, grabbed the marshal's club to keep the man from hitting him again. He struggled with the marshal and that did it! The law had all the excuse it needed. The marshal turned red in the face, you could see his eyes flash red. He was so mad, he shook. And before anyone knew what happened, he stepped back two steps, pulled out a gun and shot Clyde. Twice. In the stomach.

The whole way to the hospital in Jackson, Clyde's head lay on my lap in the back seat of Cousin Joe's car. Blood was oozing out and I was quietly begging, "Brother, please don't die, please don't die." One and one half hours later we finally arrived in Jackson. After a long wait in the waiting room, one white person came out with the word that Clyde was dead!

Dead! My brother, my hero, was dead, and anger filled my insides. All that fighting some place off in Europe didn't kill him; all that army talk about making the world a free place to live, he had come home safe from the white man's war only to be shot down six months later by a white man in his own hometown. And after the funeral, it was all over. There was nothing more to be said about it. The bigoted whites would not question the authority of the town marshal, and many of the blacks lived in silent fear.

It's hard to describe; but when we'd spent our whole lifetime with limited opportunities, spent our whole lifetime being told our place is at the bottom, we could not help but have a low image of ourselves. And after awhile, our hope or anger or whatever it s called just sorta dries up, like a muscle that never gets used. What did it matter anyway? And within several months I got enough money together to go west. Maybe California could bring a better life. And it was in fact a good choice for me at that time.

To me the depth of what bigotry and racism had done to us as a black people in the South is reflected in terms of what we had to do to begin a movement that would begin to liberate ourselves at least from the legal segregation of the South. We first had to begin to affirm ourselves and our own dignity. We had to say to ourselves that indeed black is beautiful. Now normally it ought to be the behavior of society to affirm the other person's dignity and to give other people a sense of worth. We should be able to get personal affirmation from our friends, our teachers, our mother and family, etc., so that children will not have to grow up with the uncertainty of their worth or dignity as a person. But we had to begin by affirming ourselves of our dignity because a whole society had been teaching the opposite.

Sociologists believe that the way such people will be healed is to direct their anger at the direct problem, and I believe that too. The difficulty comes in identifying the real problem. Most people will believe their problem to be other people, but in my life even as a boy, I was able to see that the basic problem that we face in this racist society was an economic problem. The person that practices bigotry is believing the end result will be economic superiority. I truly believe that behind this bigotry is economics, that in order to claim a piece of the American Dream they must prove their power through the things that they end up possessing. Having money and wealth is the sure way to prestige, influence, praise, and power. Through my observations of the system, I learned that lesson well. I found that my whole desire in life was to do that, and to get that power. I was looking for my own affirmation and I planned to get it through materialism.

MEETING JESUS

And then one morning at the age of 27, I was converted to Jesus Christ in this little mission in Pasadena. What really happened to me was that for the first time in my life, I recognized that I was loved by a holy God. I was overshadowed by God's love and I was able to see for the first time my own sinfulness in the light of a God who loved me anyway. I found out that I could confess my sins, and this good God would forgive me and accept me as His own, and it was too good to be true. It was what I had been looking for all of my life. So at my conversion then, I gave my life to this God of love and decided to follow Him completely. I began seeking ways to organize my energy in such a way as to be able to follow God and His demands in Scripture, which is still my goal for today. That morning changed my life completely.

But the struggle didn't end there. After conversion, I went back to Mississippi to live among those same bigoted people who had not yet found their personal affirmation, and it was tense. I guess for the first five or six years of our ministry in Mississippi, to a certain degree I could avoid southern white people. As much as possible I kept myself somewhat aloof from them, but then if you were a black preacher in rural Mississippi they sorta expected you not to interact with them, even though they called you "uppity." So it was easy for me to avoid the tense situations. But as the sixties came along, pretty soon I found myself having to be confronted, and I found that the pain was still there even in my life.

I suspect that it was the night in the Brandon Jail where God really began to push my own life past hatred. Twenty-three of us were almost beaten to death by the Mississippi highway patrol because of some civil rights activities in Mendenhall. That was the night that God gave me a real compassion for whites that I never before thought possible. That night when those men were beating us and brutalizing us and stomping on us, on me in particular, I saw their pain releasing itself in cold hatred even beyond their own control of stopping it. I was trying to figure out the cause of that madness and I was able to realize that their sin of bigotry had turned into a sickness of disease that poisoned their whole being. Hatred was eating at the hearts of these people like madness and their faces were so twisted with hate that they looked like white-faced demons. For the first time I saw what hate had done to those people. These policemen were poor. They saw themselves as failures. The only way they knew how to find a sense of worth was by beating us. Their racism made them feel like "somebody."

When I saw that, I just couldn't hate back. I could only pity them. I said to God that night, "God, if you will let me get out of this jail alive"—and I really didn't think I would; maybe I was trying to bargain with Him—"I really want to preach a gospel that will heal these people too." And by God's grace I did come out alive, but with a new call. My call to preach the gospel now extended to whites. I saw they needed to be set free too. I began to understand that the same gospel that frees blacks also frees whites. You can't free one without the other, for our destiny is tied together.

Those lessons were not easy to learn. My beating and the frustration and bitterness that followed took their toll. Soon after I had a heart attack and was hospitalized in Mound Bayou which was an all-black town. After a partial recovery I found myself back in the same hospital with ulcers, so I had a lot to think about lying in that hospital bed. I thought about blacks and whites. About how in a country that claimed to stand for "liberty and justice for all," a black man in Mississippi could get no justice. I thought about how in Mississippi, "Christians" were the most racist whites of all. How white preachers were in on most of the murders of civil rights leaders. How Sunday School teachers were leading members of the Klan. I thought of how the white "Christian" businessmen supported the whole economic system which exploited blacks. And there were times that I thought maybe there was only one way to go—to give up on whites and white Christians and just work for me and mine. It would be easier to just leave all that struggle behind us.

But when I was most tempted to give up, about to

decide that the gospel couldn't reconcile—at least not in Mendenhall, Mississippi—two doctors administered healing to my spirit even as they cared for my body. A white lady doctor and a young black male doctor were themselves images of hope—living examples of reconciliation. And hope began to flicker again. Even when things looked darkest, when I most wanted to run, I couldn't get away from my new call: God had called me to take the gospel to whites, too. And I could really begin to see a healing process take place in my life. God was helping me to love people without desiring anything in return. God's love for me was now beginning to flow through me. How sweet God's forgiveness and healing were! I found them to be bigger and stronger than even hatred and bigotry!

A MAN OF THE MAU MAUS

I want to share one more example of an incident when I was able to see and review how bigotry affected people. It was in 1980 when my two sons, Spencer and Derek, and I went to Kenya, East Africa, to spend a month. We spent most of our time living in the village of Kikuyu, in the region from which the Mau Maus came.

I remember we were talking one day to one of the elders in the village who also had been an officer in Kenya's liberation movement. When we found this out we wanted to know more about how this man became involved in the movement. So we went over one night and spent all night there with a tape recorder and let him talk to us. He told us what made him a Mau Mau. A Mau Mau, or Kenyan freedom fighter, would do whatever was necessary to liberate the people. And this is what he told us.

This elder said when he was a little boy they lived on a big plantation where his father was one of the house servants. All the kids in his family were also raised up to be house servants. He said there were hundreds of other Africans who lived on this giant plantation, but it was his father's job as a house servant to fix the food and do the serving. One day his father was bringing a platter of food and dishes to serve to the guests of their master, and his father accidentally dropped those platters, and all the dishes fell. He said that the master took his father out into the back and took a whip and whipped his father as he stood there and watched his father cry like a baby. There he was, a five- or six-year-old boy seeing his father become as a helpless man.

But this man grew up too and had to become a house servant because that is what he knew, and he was a servant for that same family. But by now the liberation movement in Kenya had begun, and he would hear about meetings that would be off in the forest some place, and in order to join the Mau Maus they had to go to these meetings. So he went to one of those meetings, and there he heard the talk about liberation and about how they could be men. This leader told how they didn't have to be children any more. The European society had made the African males boys, children, second class citizens, and now they needed to stand up and be men. The group was told what it would take to be a man and to throw off that inferiority. He said that if you wanted to join the Mau Maus as part of his liberation movement, that you had to go back and kill your master and his family, and then when you did that you could come back and join the Mau Maus.

What they did was they took a large cup and they cut their wrists and allowed so much blood to run into that cup from each one of their wrists, until the cup was full of blood from the people who were in the room. Then they stirred that blood and then they all drank that blood together. That was the oath that one had to take, and the idea was that they had all been joined together by blood; and the only thing that would separate them now was death. If anyone went out and shared any information about the movement, he was as good as dead. This old gentleman said he left that evening and went out and killed his masters and their family, then he went out and joined the secret society of the Mau Maus. He also said that this was the first time that he ever shared this story with anyone.

NEEDED: GOD'S LOVE

And again, I saw firsthand the deadliness and the hatred of bigotry and what it can do to people. And I believe that the only real cure for hatred and bigotry is that we as individuals respond in obedience to God's Word. We do have a responsibility and we as individuals can make a response in terms of loving, caring, and affirming the dignity of those we meet.

But also, we must create a community of people where that affirmation takes place. That is one of the greatest needs in Northwest Pasadena where I live. We need to become a people who can soak up the hatred and anger of society, and let it end with us instead of reacting to it and passing it on to others. We need not respond to the hatred and violence with more hatred and violence, but rather penetrate that cover with love and compassion and concern. And of course that takes God's love and power at work inside of us!

In closing, think about the needs and opportunities for a ministry of reconciliation in your own community. Determine what two groups of people in your community might have the greatest need for reconciliation. What part can you play?

8

It's a Matter of Life and Death!

Eric Pement

"Which do you think is more valuable—an unborn eagle, or an unborn baby?" A pro-life group asks this question, and then points to an unusual statistic:

The penalty for killing an unborn eagle in this country is a fine of up to $5000, and up to five years in prison. But killing an unborn baby is not considered a crime at all, as long as the mother approves.

In fact, under certain circumstances, a doctor who does *not* advise a woman to abort her baby can be sued for hundreds of thousands of dollars. About 4,500 unborn children are aborted (i.e., killed or terminated) in this country every *day*. Most of these are healthy children without any mental or physical disabilities, but are simply viewed as an unwanted burden.

However, the possibility of raising a disabled child is frightening to many parents. So much so that Dr. Francis Crick and Dr. James Watson, who won the Nobel prize for discovering DNA, have recommended that a baby not be declared "fully human" until three days after its birth, so that its parents might legally destroy it if it appears defective.

LIFE: A VERY TOUCHY SUBJECT

Why are people so touchy when it comes to abortion? I've seen good friends and family members, who like to gab about anything and everything, refuse to discuss abortion for fear of having an argument. Abortion is a super-sensitive matter because it strikes at the heart of what it means to be human. If the fetus isn't really human, then killing it is no more significant than killing a chicken or a puppy. But if the unborn child *is* human, then killing it is murder.

The same uneasy feelings pop up when people are asked hard questions about infanticide (the killing of infants) and euthanasia ("mercy killing"). Parents may consider infanticide after they find their newborn baby has severe birth defects or is profoundly retarded. What if the child will be bedridden the rest of its life? Relatives may contemplate "mercy killing" of an adult who is terminally ill or who may be permanently comatose though still alive.

One day, we may have to decide whether to take a life. Any decision like this demands careful reasoning and the ability to see through faulty arguments. Just because a person has a college degree doesn't mean he or she can reach the right conclusions. One may have a good memory for details but lack common sense. Moreover, if you start with the wrong assumptions about life, you'll end up with the wrong conclusions.

Any decision we come to about the sanctity (sacredness) of life should not be determined by what our friends might think of us. Whether "most people" agree or disagree on the sanctity of life is not important. In the final analysis, we should be led by medical evidence, careful reason, and the written Word of God. A moral decision to stand for right and wrong may be unpopular, but in the long run that's the only thing that will satisfy your conscience before yourself and before God.

WHY TAKE INNOCENT LIFE?

The reasons people support abortion, infanticide, and euthanasia are far more numerous than we could list here. Scores of books have been written defending the right to abort, as well as defending the right of the unborn to remain unharmed. I've heard a dozen arguments for eliminating the unborn or defective child, but most of them revolve around two main points:

1. The first is usually called "quality of life." It says, how can life be worth living if you're severely crippled? If a child or an adult becomes so profoundly retarded that he doesn't even know his own name, the person isn't even as good as an animal. For one family to face the medical expenses of caring for a "human vegetable" or a "basket case" (someone missing all four limbs) is just too much. Also, even if society could afford the high costs, suppose the baby's mother didn't want him or love him? It would be better for all concerned if the child were aborted or dead. (A similar argument is used to support euthanasia.)

2. The second main point, which usually applies to

abortion, is "freedom of choice." It says the choice to bear a child or to abort should be left up to the mother.

This idea is expressed in a number of ways: "Well, abortion isn't anything for anybody to pass judgment on but me." "A woman should have the right to control her own body and determine her own future." "It's my body, it's my life." "If you don't believe in abortion, you don't have to have one, but don't tell me *I* can't have one."

If you examine these statements carefully, you'll see they are different ways of arguing for freedom of choice. Sometimes these arguments can sound awfully convincing.

STEPS ON THE LADDER OF LOGIC

To judge abortion wisely, we must approach it by examining the fundamentals. In fact, this method should be used when you're trying to understand any difficult subject, not just abortion.

First, consider the basic values, the fundamental issues at stake. What's at the heart of the matter? Question the *principles,* not the program. Next, determine which values or principles should take priority over other values. (One sure way of knowing which principles are more important is by studying what the Bible says.) Look at the exceptions last.

Although exceptions may occur, an exception—a rare, one-in-a-million case—should never force you to toss out a rule which is good 99 percent of the time. Likewise, a fact which is questionable or trivial should never be used to overthrow or "cross out" a fact which is solidly proven and well-established. (For example, just because scientists can't figure out how the honeybee is able to fly doesn't make all of aeronautics worthless.)

We'll use the step-by-step method in dealing with the sanctity of life. We begin with the foundational question of human beings—why are people important? The answer to this question will set the stage. The next step is to examine the unborn fetus—is it alive, is it human, is it significant? Finally, we'll talk about the "hard cases"—when might it be permissible to take away the life of an unborn child?

WHAT ARE PEOPLE REALLY WORTH?

If life came about by a chance accident, and human beings are nothing more than two-legged mobile "computers" using carbon cells instead of silicon chips, then why shouldn't we treat people like machines? Machines have no "rights"—we can chop them up, sell them, or destroy them if they fail to live up to our desires.

However, human beings possess a wholly different character than anything else on earth. Not just because we are alive: plants are alive. Not just because we are social beings: ants and fish are social beings. Not just because we can think: chimpanzees and computers can think (well, maybe one day!).

Humans are unique because we were created by God and bear God's image. From the greatest Einstein to the drunk in the gutter, each person carries a spiritual nature which comes from God—a soul, a character which bears the imprint of the Creator. In Genesis 1:27 we find that God created mankind, both male and female, in His own image. This "image" was not erased by Adam and Eve; according to James, we still retain God's "likeness" (Jas. 3:9).

To most of the world, people's importance depends on who they know, what they can do, and how much they possess. But in the eyes of God, each person is of enormous importance. God does not value us because of our looks, our strength, our I.Q., or our money; He loves each person individually. Each person is unique and has value, even if that person is "unwanted" by his friends or "unloved" by her mother. Jesus Christ loves that person regardless.

Each person has a right to life, even if he or she can't "contribute" to society. Jesus identified Himself with the outcast, not with the in-crowd, when He said, "Whatever you did for one of the *least* of these my brothers, you did for me" (Matt. 25:40, emphasis added). God is no respecter of persons—He does not play favorites (Acts 10:34; Eph. 6:9)—and His regard for people is not based on their social or intellectual capacities.

WHAT IS THE UNBORN CHILD?

Although some people can look at this question and say, "Easy answer!" other people have difficulty with it. For some people, the unborn child is just "fetal tissue" or a "product of conception." The implication of such language is that the unborn baby is something less than human.

A few people dislike calling the fetus a "baby" because they don't believe it's alive. Even the U.S. Supreme Court in its famous 1973 abortion decision (Roe v. Wade) said it couldn't resolve "the difficult question of when human life begins."

However, medical doctors, biology teachers, and even most abortionists admit that life begins at conception. Indeed, ten years before the Supreme Court's abortion decision, Planned Parenthood distributed a pamphlet which stated clearly, "An abortion kills the life of a baby after it has begun."

This can be seen fairly easily.

The same standards for life, used for plants and animals at any level of complexity, can be used to show that a fertilized egg or a developing fetus do indeed qualify as "life." The difference between a dead body and a live one is not whether it has DNA or is made up of cells, but whether it carries out certain biological functions. These basic life functions would include consumption of food, metabolism, respiration, elimination of waste, growth and movement, and the capacity to reproduce when the organism reaches maturity. This is how biologists and most dictionaries define "life."

You don't have to be a biochemist to recognize that the embryo carries on all the functions of life from the moment of conception. A simple thing to remember is that if the fetus weren't alive, it wouldn't grow and move.

Is the fetus a human life?

Well, it's certainly not *plant* life! And I don't know too many people who would claim it's a form of bird or reptile life.

On a more serious note, we all know the unborn child is not fully grown, is immature, and so on. But the humanity of an unborn baby can never be doubted, just as the "birdness" of an unborn eagle should never be doubted.

But there's more. Biological evidences for the humanity of the unborn child, however true they may be, still do not convey the whole story.

The Scripture gives the view that can never be seen by biology and medicine. In it, God reveals that He has a plan for each person's life, and that He is involved in our growth and development from the very beginning.

In the book of Psalms, King David describes his creation by God: "For you created my inmost being; you knit me together in my mother's womb. I praise you because I am fearfully and wonderfully made; your works are wonderful, I know that full well. My frame was not hidden from you when I was made in the secret place. When I was woven together in the depths of the earth, your eyes saw my unformed body. All the days ordained for me were written in your book before one of them came to be" (Ps. 139:13-16).

Seen in this light, the unborn child is not merely a developing human organism (though the baby *is* that, of course). God declares that He has also ordained a purpose and a course of life for that child, standing behind the child's formation in the womb long before it is born.

Now, after looking at the Bible's estimate of human life, and especially the value of unborn children, we can examine the main arguments for abortion in their proper perspective.

WHEN SHOULD LIFE BE TAKEN AWAY?

One final tip on clear thinking: don't let anyone snow you into thinking that because something is *legal*, then it must be *right*. The two are not the same. It's legal in this country to be a drunk, a pornographer, a racist, and a Satanist. In Nazi Germany, it was once legal to kill Jews. However, just because something is permissible under national law doesn't mean it's acceptable in the eyes of God.

Now, what about abortion and infanticide?

If humans are made in God's image and life is a special gift given to us by God, and if unborn children are truly human, then the basic idea of abortion is wrong for the same reason murder is wrong. God gives life to humans, and He forbids the murder of innocent people (see Deut. 27:25). If we have no right to kill people simply because they are ugly, poor, or of the "wrong" color or language, then how can we justify killing people because they inconvenience us financially or do not meet our standards for intelligence?

I have seen severely deformed children, "basket cases" by some people's standards. It is their *humanity* that gives them value, not their marketable skills or their "quality of life." People have intrinsic value simply because they are human, regardless of what they may be capable of by earthly standards.

But what about freedom of choice?

Certainly, we know that both men and women have a right to freedom of choice. The United States Declaration of Independence put it this way: that among the rights God has given man are the right to "life, liberty, and the pursuit of happiness." To a certain extent, this right to liberty includes freedom of speech, of religion, of assembly, of occupation, and of things which pertain to a person's future.

However, the right to personal liberty has limits. We cannot shout "fire" in a crowded theater, we cannot assemble to overthrow the government, and we may not exercise our rights in a way that endangers or restricts someone else's rights. In short, there is a priority of rights, which is summed up in this maxim: "Your rights end where my nose begins."

One of the arguments for "choice" in having an abortion is that a woman has a right to control her own body. To a certain degree, this is true. However, the unborn child is not part of the woman's body. It has its *own* body, with its own DNA (quite different from the mother's), its own fingerprints (visible at three months), and its own independent heart and bloodstream. Sometimes, even the blood type is different! So while a woman may have the right to her own life and liberty, that doesn't give her the right to take away her child's life.

An objection which comes up quite often is, "You may not believe in abortion, but at least give the mother the freedom to decide for herself." But in the case of abortion, what this is asking for is the choice to save or kill an unborn baby. Under the normal course of law, we do not give the choice to kill innocent people into the hands of anybody.

Maybe this illustration will help.

In the United States 150 years ago, slavery was acceptable in some states and the black slave was not considered a true "person." The Southern states argued that each state should be free to choose for itself whether to permit slavery. They told the North, "If you don't believe in slavery, you can outlaw slavery in your state. But don't impose your values on us."

The United States eventually reached the breaking point on this issue, culminating in the Civil War. Although our national conscience was dim for years on the subject of slavery, it was eventually provoked to see that human rights superseded financial benefit. No doubt the slaveholders supposed that their "majority vote" gave them a right to own slaves. Unfortunately, this interpretation of "choice" took away the life and liberty of millions of human beings.

One of the final problems of the "freedom of choice" argument is that it sees only two possibilities. Either abort, or be stuck with a baby the rest of your life. This is not true; there are more than two options. The mother could give the baby up for adoption, which would seem to be far more humane than aborting it.

WHAT ABOUT THE HARD CASES?

Would abortion be acceptable following a case of rape?

As evil and as hateful as rape is, killing the innocent party is not the answer. The baby was not guilty of any crime. The child's conception may have come about through an evil act, but the child itself is not evil and has the same potential for good as any human being. In the rare instance where bearing a baby normally would endanger the health of the mother (sometimes a rape victim is young), special medical treatment to preserve both mother and child should be sought.

A very hard decision must be made when a pregnancy would literally kill the mother. For example, such a case might be an ectopic (or "tubal") pregnancy, or perhaps the discovery of uterine cancer, where an immediate hysterectomy is needed. If the baby continues to grow, both mother and child will die.

On such occasions, where we are faced with two certain deaths (unless God miraculously intervenes), the only alternative is to abort the child. An innocent life is still taken, though we should seek to save the child if at all possible.

The *ideal* solution would be to move a tubally-implanted fetus to a safe location within the uterus. Currently, we cannot move the fetus without killing it, but as medical technology advances, this may become possible in the future.

CONSISTENCY AND COMPASSION

To sum up then, a consistent view of abortion, infanticide, and mercy killing is one which begins from the most basic platform—the value of human beings. Then, with compassion we try to work out the best way to solve human problems, while safeguarding human life.

Sometimes, two things will come into conflict, such as a woman's right to be free from the cost and burden of pregnancy, and the child's right to live. Obviously, if a wife is unready or unwilling to become a mother, the time to make that decision is before the baby is conceived. She and her husband should take steps to prevent conception.

In the same light, if a woman is unmarried, if she would follow the Bible's instruction to "flee from sexual immorality" (1 Cor. 6:18) and remain sexually pure, most of the problems of unwanted pregnancy (and most of the reasons for abortion) would be solved. This does not let the men off the hook, though—the problem of abortion is a national sin, and the male's responsibility for this sin is at *least* equal to the woman's, if not greater.

When people have fallen into sexual sin and a child has been conceived in the process, the answer is not to tell the mother to escape the consequences of the sin by killing the child, thus committing a greater sin. The Christian response is to respect the new life which has been created, recognize that it has as much a right to live as any of us do, and do what we can to aid both mother and child in building a new life.

Abortion will probably never be an easy thing to talk about. But if we'll remember that we're talking about people's lives and ultimate values, those discussions will become a little less frightening and a little more important.

9

Media:
Truth and Trash

Tom Finley

The girl looked at her reflection in her bedroom mirror. Her image was dark, tan from the intense sun rays that baked the high-altitude village.

She was not a beautiful girl, she thought to herself. There were no beautiful girls in her town. Everyone looked the same: dark skin, dark eyes, black hair, and round, almost plump, faces.

Had she been born a hundred years sooner, she would have thought that the whole world was populated with dark, round people. But she knew better, she sighed to herself.

Turning from the wall mirror, she grabbed a magazine from the dresser and flopped herself down on her bed. She held a Spanish-language version of one of the famous French fashion magazines. In a rural land with almost no television, magazines are the chief source of visual information about the outside world. In her country, as in all the surrounding South American countries, the foreign language editions of the American and French fashion magazines are among the hottest selling items.

She propped her pillow against the headboard, leaned back into the feathery softness, and drew up her knees so she could rest the magazine against her legs.

The woman on the cover seemed to return the girl's intense gaze. The woman was beautiful. Light brown hair with blonde highlights cascaded in loose curls to the model's shoulders. Green eyes, eyes that grabbed hold of the girl's gaze and wouldn't let go. White skin on a thin face. Red lips.

It was the high cheekbones and the long, thin nose that captivated the young girl. She delicately touched the tips of her fingers to the woman's cheekbones. She put her fingers to her own face, felt the wide, fleshy nose, touched the cheekbones.

There was a man in one of the huge cities on the coast. A doctor. She had read about him in a fashion magazine. He was very famous. People came to him from all over South America. Like magic, he could change their faces. With a knife, he could tighten the skin, lengthen the nose, raise the cheekbones.

She would bring the cover photo to him. He would help her. She would be beautiful!

• • • • •

This story is true. Literally thousands of rural South American women and girls have invested great sums of money in the futile attempt to appear "European." North Americans also spend money for face lifts, "tummy tucks," hair transplants, suction removal of fat from thighs, and other "improvements."

It is a very interesting phenomenon, a glimpse into some of the silliness of human nature. In response to a flood of fashion magazines, ordinary looking (not ugly, just ordinary) people are now willing to submit themselves to the pain and expense of cosmetic surgery. And why? So they can return to their villages or their big city neighborhoods with high cheekbones and razor-thin beaks. It goes to show the influence the media, whether print or electronic, can have on people.

In order to cover this topic properly, we must consider three important facets of the subject: the *extent of the influence* that the mass media have on people like you and me; the *source* of the messages we receive from the media; and the proper way to *separate truth from trash*.

Let's define "mass media" as those channels of communication which sway or influence our thinking, and which are widespread enough so that all of us have experienced them. Is that definition too complex? Well, let's say that mass media can be defined as radio, TV, and commercials. It's more than that, of course, but we'll be busy enough just talking about these three!

THE EXTENT OF THE INFLUENCE

Think back to the young girl in the mountain village reading her fashion magazine. There are two factors that jump out at me as I think of her experience.

The first factor is the *attractiveness* of the magazine's

message. That magazine and all the others print beautiful people on their covers. Television shows, commercials, and music videos also throw great-looking people at us. And the message *is* attractive! The people look like they have it together. The life of a rock star seems exciting! Being a Hollywood celeb sounds fun! Why be a boring face in a boring crowd when you can—according to one TV commercial—drink a certain beer and suddenly life's a party?

The message is exciting and attractive, and this explains the incredible extent of the media's influence. People who work with kids see a lot of fads sweep through a group. One year it was Calvin Kleins. Not because "Calvins" are better made, but because they had a sexy commercial. One summer all the guys in one group had to have "Mach 7" Boogie boards. None of the reasonably priced boards would do. Any poor sap who owned anything less than a Mach 7 was made to feel like a dirtball. (The funny thing is, nobody in that crowd was any good at riding Boogie boards anyway!) Even I am not without guilt. After watching the premier episode of "Miami Vice," I ran down to the store and bought a white jacket with the cuffs rolled up! (By the time you read this, millions of similar jackets will probably have been worn and now long forgotten. Maybe even "Miami Vice" will be long forgotten!)

There is another factor to consider as we look at the media's influence. It could be called the time factor. It relates to the *amount* of influential information we receive from the media. The South American girl spent a great deal of time reading her magazines. In our country, the average household has a TV running seven hours a day!

Are you a couch potato? A couch potato is a person who stares for hours as the television screen flicks its images into the front room. Believe it or not, the nation is filling up with couch potatoes—with mashed potato minds.

As research for an article, a youth pastor once watched 70 minutes of television and counted the number of commercials aired. Are you ready? More than 40 commercials in just over an hour! Forty! Think of the thousands upon thousands of commercials you see in a month's viewing time. If you are an average high school age Christian and a television viewer, you spend about 25 hours a week in school. You attend 4 hours or less of church each week. But you watch up to 40 hours of television. Just as the strongest dog wins the dogfight, the amount of time you place yourself under the influence of a particular set of messages determines which message is the most important factor in swaying your thinking.

Market analysts are people who earn big bucks researching and predicting what products and promotional techniques will beep our buttons. At this writing there is a TV commercial that is the obvious result of market research. It is for a breakfast cereal, and it takes a very sensitive subject and exploits it to sell flakes. Somewhere some market analyst realized the great fear that many members of the public have of cancer. Now that the disease known as AIDS has crossed over into the general population, people are even more frightened by the prospect of contracting cancer. So what does the breakfast cereal do? It shows a healthy young "Yuppie" woman explaining how doctors think a high fiber diet may help to prevent cancer. Then she says that there is no proof to support this but, just in case, she will evermore eat the contents of the box she holds up to the camera. This is manipulation of the basest kind. Why eat this cereal? Because you will get cancer if you don't. That is the subconscious message the ad is trying to instill in us. What a great thought to start off each morning! But the commercial sells cereal. People respond to mass media influence.

How responsive are you? Let's find out. Here are some quiz questions.

1. Would you pay $40 for a popular brand name jeans rather than $20 for the same jeans without the designer label and the pocket designs?

2. When you take a shower, do you pretend you are on stage performing the latest hit single? (Showerheads make great microphones.) And do you wish you could be like that stage star you are imitating?

3. When you were a little kid, did you hold your breath and turn blue until your mom bought you the latest toy you had seen on TV?

4. Do you tend to repeat certain phrases and mannerisms that your favorite TV personalities use? Did you ever buy a Mr. T doll?

Obviously these questions are tongue-in-cheek. Yet they are based on what really happens. People *are* changed and influenced by what they watch and hear.

Here is a serious question: Have you ever seen a person murdered? Probably not. But by the age of 10, virtually everyone in the Free World has witnessed hundreds of deaths and murders on TV and at the movies. The media, particularly television, have given us all common experiences that we would not otherwise have had. Because of television, someone in the Yukon "knows" Bill Cosby as well as someone in Florida does.

I live by the beach. You may happen to live by a wheatfield, something I've never done. Yet I know enough about wheatfields from watching TV to have a pretty good idea what living next to a field of wheat is like. And if you watch ABC sports, you probably have learned a bit about what it's like to ride a Hawaiian wave. So you and I are more alike than we would ever have been without the shared experience of TV. The point here is that even if you try to resist manipulation by the media, you are still changed by the media.

Some changes are for the better, of course. If you like to listen to music on the radio or record player, chances are you've attempted to learn to play some sort of musical instrument. How many talented musicians and composers would never have wanted to make music if they had never heard music? This is something positive that the mass market recording medium has done.

But just as there is a flip side to any record, there is another side to the media's influence. For instance, the positive effects of popular music can be largely offset by the worldly, immoral messages of some of the lyrics. And that brings us to the second important facet of our subject.

CONSIDER THE SOURCE

"The walls of the town were well built, yea, so fast and firm were they knit and compacted together, that, had it not been for the townsmen themselves, they could not have been shaken or broken for ever. For here lay the excellent wisdom of him that had built Mansoul, that the walls could never be broken down nor hurt, unless the townsmen gave consent thereto.

"This famous town of Mansoul had five gates, at which to come out, and at which to go in; and these were likewise answerable to the walls, to wit, impregnable, and such as could never be opened nor forced, but by the will and leave of those within. The names of the gates are these: Ear-gate, Eye-gate, Mouth-gate, Nose-gate, and Feel-gate."

Like the city of Mansoul, described by John Bunyan in

his *Holy War,* written about 300 years ago, people have "walls and gates" designed to protect us from outside enemies while at the same time enabling us to perceive the world around us. Bunyan, with great insight, shows us that, first of all, there is something to protect ourselves from (in his story, Satan), and second that we have the power to open or close the gates to outside influence. As we consider the source of the media's messages, remember that we can shut the gates if we need to.

If the mass media were an ice cream cone, the sources of the various messages would be three flavors of ice cream.

Flavor number one is the world. The world is secular, that is, not particularly biblical. It includes the philosophies and ethics of non-Christian society. Although some of the ethics of the world may be sound and true, in the broad view the world is very wrong. If the world were indeed ice cream, it would leave a bitter taste in the Christian's mouth. But the problem is, the more of this ice cream one eats, the better it tastes. Many Christian kids fall slowly away from God as they sink their teeth deeper and deeper into the cone. You see, the world can be a very attractive place, and the glamour of the world—the money, the fame, the life-styles—can be a sugary trap. But as you know, you can only lick this ice cream so long before it licks you.

The second source of messages vying for your attention is Satan. For our purpose here, let's define the difference between the world and Satan as a degree of subtlety. The world is subtly evil, Satan is blatant. (There's much more to it than this, of course, but let's keep it simple.) In a sense, the subtle influence of the world should scare us more than the blatantly obvious influence of the devil himself. (Like you, I hate Satan and avoid him whenever I recognize his presence. But the world is easier to live with. Know what I mean? Its toned-down evil can slip in through the tiny cracks in my defensive gates.) To return to the ice cream analogy, the world's ice cream is bitter and will slowly make one sick, while Satan's ice cream is fast-acting poison.

Because Satan is so blatant, it's rather easy for anyone who knows the Bible to recognize his influence on the media. Let me give you a personal example: my pastor and I have a bit of a running disagreement on the horrors of secular Punk rock. We both feel that it is blatantly evil. He feels that it is one of the worst perverters of today's youth. He mentions this from the pulpit every chance he gets. I, on the other hand, don't really give a rip about Punk. Why don't I? Because the lyrics are so obviously stupid. And because they are so obviously stupid, it is easy to show a young Christian, even a punker, how dumb it really is. (Full tilt Punk seems to be on the way out anyway.)

In comparison television is much more dangerous! It is subtle and worldly, and it is hard to convince television watchers that they are glued to something that, in the long run, may do them great spiritual damage. At the risk of sounding like a member of the lunatic fringe, I would like to point out that Walt Disney may have done more to mess up the members of my generation (kids of the sixties) than our rock and roll heroes ever did! What, ol' Walt? It's possible.

Look at those great old movies Disney made in the 1960s. You know, the family pictures with a middle class mom and dad with squeaky-clean kids. Nothing wrong here, right? Ah, but look at the plots. Every movie had the same plot. Dumb old mom and dad tell the kids not to do something. But the kids go ahead and do it anyway, sneaky-like, and in so doing they catch the kidnappers or the bank robbers, or they save the farm or the kitty cat or whatever. By the end of the film, the kids are heroes and mom and dad are proud parents.

But what is the message here? Subtly, the message is that it is OK to disobey your parents! Don't listen to mom and dad, because you really are the smart one! Did the members of my generation buy into this philosophy? You better believe we did. On a subconscious level. That is why the subtle poison is the dangerous one.

Yet we seldom hear our pastors preach about the evils of television. Why? Perhaps because everyone watches it, and it's hard to admit to ourselves that we are addicted to a poison.

The reason to worry about the low-key worldly influence rather than the obviously Satanic is easy to describe: a drowning man only can be rescued when he realizes he is drowning and responds to offers of aid. Christians who buy into the world through the hard-to-pin-down evil influence of television, music, and so on, rarely realize that they are drowning spiritually.

We must therefore learn to recognize when we are receiving trash. We'll get to that in the third part of our discussion, but let's take one last bite out of our ice cream cone.

The final source of media messages is Christian. There are Christian radio and TV stations, and there are Christian programs and records on secular stations. Even MTV is starting to show a few of the better Christian rock videos. But the Christian influence is tiny. The chances of a friend of yours turning on the TV to a random station at a random time and finding anything truly biblical are pretty slim. Incidentally, keep in mind that even though someone on the radio or TV appears to be Christian, he or she may not really be biblically sound. There are a few nuts in the Christian ice cream!

So what do we do? Do we turn off all the radios, televisions, cassettes, and compact disks? Well, yes! That'd be a really good idea! But since none of us wants to do that, let's talk about a few practical steps we can take to insure that the media messages are not turning us into spiritual munchkins.

SEPARATING TRUTH FROM TRASH

The key word is *filter*. Just as an aquarium has a filter to screen out the dirt that would kill the fish, each Christian must develop some sort of screening method to separate truth from trash.

It is your responsibility to devise your own filter. You want it to be as accurate as possible, that is, you want whatever influence the media has on you to be helpful and positive. As you grow and mature in a world filled with the constant barrage of media messages, you want to take the good that will broaden and deepen your character. You want to ignore the bad that will harden your spiritual heart.

There are three steps to developing an accurate filter. First, recognize that the Bible is God's foundation of truth upon which you must build your life. Second, don't believe everything you hear from the media. Third, consider the source.

Let's take a look at that last one first. *Consider the source*. The main source of the media messages is the world, and therefore, indirectly or directly, Satan. The philosophies of the world—the glitter, the glamour, going for the gusto, and all that—simply cannot accurately reflect the entirety of God's truth, because they are not of God. That does not mean that the world cannot stumble upon true and important things. For example, many starving people in the Third World have received assistance from North Americans because the media alerted us to the plight. This is a good thing. Thank God that television and newspapers showed us the pictures of dying millions. We were spurred into action. Yet that does not alter the fact that the media and the messages are fundamentally of the world. Therefore, we Christians must never forget to compare what we watch and hear to God's Word.

So the first step to building an accurate and reliable filter is to understand that the messages we receive from the media are normally not worth much. The source—the world—simply does not measure up to God.

The second step is not to believe everything we see and hear. Remember the girl who dreamed of cosmetic surgery? She probably had no idea that the cover photo she so adored had been retouched, altered to make the model look better than real life. Almost all photographs published in high quality books and periodicals are "dot etched" or even highlighted with an airbrush. Dot etching is a process which eliminates blemishes on, say, the model's face and balances her skin tone. Airbrushing adds shadows (or removes them) to make her cheekbones appear higher. Chemical processing turns her ordinary green eyes into pools of luminescence. In short, the vast majority of pretty faces are just a bit plastic.

It has been said that Paul Simon's old song about Kodachrome giving nice bright colors and making all the world a sunny day is commenting on the fact that we are all sucked into believing the world is a better place than it really is. It's like the tinsel on a Christmas tree. The tinsel looks bright and valuable, like strands of silver or gold. But it is worthless. Keep that in mind when your favorite rock performer advocates indiscriminate sex or beating up your enemies. The advice might sound nice, but it has little substance. (Keep in mind, too, that the rocker had to spend ten years locked in a bedroom to learn how to play guitar. He or she probably knows less about wise living than you do!) So cast a critical eye on all you see.

The final step is really the whole foundation of filter-building. *Recognize that the Bible is God's truth,* a rock to which you must anchor your life.

The Bible shows us what life actually is all about. It shows us reality. It is a model to which you can compare all the information you receive from the mass media. If the television says something that agrees with the Bible, fine. If the two disagree, trash the TV.

This brings up a very important consideration. In order to use the Bible as a tool to compare truth and trash, you *must know the Bible well.* Without it, you are completely on your own in this world. God's wisdom is far above the world's, but yours isn't. If you try to run your life without God's wisdom, you will fail. (If I could spend time with you personally, the one thing in all the universe I would try to communicate to you is the importance of knowing God's Word!) Some say they believe in God but don't study the Bible. How can a person truly believe in Someone they know almost nothing about? Read your Bible. Attend Bible studies. Plan on spending the rest of your life next to a well-worn copy of God's message.

Again, the Bible is a model. It reveals the world as it really is. As a globe describes the world, the Bible describes the world that God created. The mass media present a different model. Like a "globe" in the shape of a cube, it is not accurate.

Filter the messages you receive through a biblical filter. Measure. Compare. And don't believe everything the world tells you. If you do these things, you will be able to separate the truth from the trash, the good from the bad, the important from that which has no importance.

And that is the mark of a mature person.

Here are some important verses that will help you create a quality filter:

God's Spirit guides us in understanding

"We have not received the spirit of the world but the Spirit who is from God, that we may understand what God has freely given us."

1 Corinthians 2:12

"The Spirit of truth. The world cannot accept him, because it neither sees him nor knows him. But you know him, for he lives in you and will be in you."

John 14:17

"But when he, the Spirit of truth, comes, he will guide you into all truth. He will not speak on his own; he will speak only what he hears, and he will tell you what is yet to come."

John 16:13

God's wisdom versus the world's wisdom

"For the wisdom of this world is foolishness in God's sight."

1 Corinthians 3:19

The unpolluted Christian

"Religion that God our Father accepts as pure and faultless is this: to look after orphans and widows in their distress and to keep oneself from being polluted by the world."

James 1:27

Friend of the world

"Anyone who chooses to be a friend of the world becomes an enemy of God."

James 4:4

"Do not love the world or anything in the world. If anyone loves the world, the love of the Father is not in him."

1 John 2:15

The power of Bible knowledge

"The word of God is living and active. Sharper than any double-edged sword, it penetrates even to dividing soul and spirit, joints and marrow; it judges the thoughts and attitudes of the heart."

Hebrews 4:12

"Let the word of Christ dwell in you richly as you teach and admonish . . . with all wisdom."

Colossians 3:16

"All Scripture is God-breathed and is useful for teaching, rebuking, correcting and training in righteousness, so that the man of God may be thoroughly equipped for every good work."

2 Timothy 3:16,17

Living a revolutionary life

"Do not conform any longer to the pattern of this world, but be transformed by the renewing of your mind."

Romans 12:2

The Acid Test

Here is perhaps the best verse in the Bible for providing an "acid test" to what the media shows or tells you:

"Finally, brothers, whatever is true, whatever is noble, whatever is right, whatever is pure, whatever is lovely, whatever is admirable—if anything is excellent or praiseworthy—think about such things."

Philippians 4:8

The verse lists eight "measuring sticks" with which we can judge any mass media message:

TRUE—Does the message agree with the Bible?

NOBLE—Does the message possess outstanding qualities and does it lead us to become better persons?

RIGHT—Does the message actively take a stand for fairness, justice, rightness?

PURE—Is the message a difficult-to-untangle combination of truth and trash?

LOVELY—Would it embarrass us if other Christians found out we listened to the message?

ADMIRABLE—Is the message something we would

want to repeat for the benefit of others?

EXCELLENT—Is it better than what we could be listening to?

PRAISEWORTHY—Is God pleased with us when we listen to the message?

If what the media says stands up to Philippians 4:8, then go ahead and enjoy it.

10

Church and State

David Edwards

Should Christians obey the law and the instructions of government authorities? Take your time before answering; there's more to this question than you might think.

PART I: THE QUESTION: MUST WE ALWAYS OBEY THE GOVERNMENT?

What Paul Says in Romans 13

In the thirteenth chapter of his epistle to the Romans, Paul makes statements about our Christian duty to obey the government that for nearly two thousand years have caused great confusion and debate among Christians:

Let every person be in subjection to the governing authorities. For there is no authority
except from God, and those which exist are established by God. Therefore he who resists authority
has opposed the ordinance of God . . . . Rulers are
not a cause of fear for good behavior, but for evil.
Do you want to have no fear of authority? Do what
is good, and you will have praise from the same;
for it is a minister of God to you for good. But if
you do what is evil, be afraid; for it does not bear
the sword for nothing; for it is a minister of God,
an avenger who brings wrath upon the one who
practices evil . . . . Because of this you also pay
taxes, for rulers are servants of God . . . . Render
to all what is due them: tax to whom tax is due;
custom to whom custom, fear to whom fear;
honor to whom honor (Rom. 13:1-7, *NASB*).

In Hebrews 13:17 these instructions are repeated:
"Obey your leaders and submit to them" *(NASB)*. And the
apostle Peter says, "Submit yourselves for the Lord's
sake to every human institution" (1 Pet. 2:13), *NASB*).

So What's the Problem?

Why have these statements caused such great difficulty? First, and most troubling, they seem to contradict
other parts of the Bible. Second, we can all immediately
think of certain evil governments that surely ought *not* to
be obeyed. Peter, when commanded by a pagan government to stop preaching the gospel, replied, "We must
obey God rather than men" (Acts 5:29). Shadrach,
Meshach, and Abed-nego, when ordered to bow down to

the idols of King Nebuchadnezzar, responded, "We are not going to serve your gods or worship the golden image that you have set up" (Dan. 3:18, *NASB*). The prophet Daniel refused to obey King Darius' law prohibiting him from praying to the God of Israel (see Dan. 6:10). In all these instances of civil defiance God showed His approval with miracles of deliverance.

It seems clear enough from these passages that God expects us to do just as Peter said, obey God rather than men. We know very well that we are not to bow down to any other god; the second commandment says so. Similarly, we cannot obey a law that forbids our prayers. And since Jesus commands us to preach the gospel in every land, His instructions will certainly take precedence over any earthly law that says otherwise.

So far it sounds fairly simple; our formula for balancing Romans 13 with the rest of the Bible will be this: We will obey the laws of the land, but only if those man-made laws do not contradict God's laws. End of discussion? No. Unfortunately, it's not that simple. A formula like that will quickly put us into a quandary from which we're unlikely ever to find our way out.

To see why, let's apply our formula to the Ten Commandments (God's laws) and the Constitution of the United States (human laws). Number one, "You shall have no other gods before Me" (Exod. 20:3, *NASB*). Whoops! We've already run into a tricky question! In America we worship our Constitution! That is, we invest it with an authority that extends over every other authority. Our Constitution is the very last word on all matters of national policy, even when those matters involve questions of morality.

This document is more a part of everyday life for our judges and lawyers than the Bible is for many Christians.

Every law in every law book in our nation is ultimately subject to this one question: "Is it constitutional?" (not, "Is it biblical?"). Anyone who holds public office in America must be willing to swear (ironically, with one hand on the Bible) to support the Constitution. By this arrangement, the office-holder may be promising *to put God second in line* to our system of government. But, because it is man-made, it frequently contradicts the Bible.

Our courts declare it lawful, for example, to kill unborn babies anytime we find it convenient to do so. China has a similar law, but she has gone one step further; there, unborn babies are killed whenever the *government* deems it necessary. And the citizens are expected to cooperate.

So a Christian husband in China might take one look at Romans 13 and say, "Phooey! I'm not going to get into *my* rickshaw and drive *my* wife and unborn child down to the local government abortion parlor! If I'm disobeying the Bible, then so be it! *I* say it's wrong to deliver my own children into the hands of murderers. And for that matter, so does God!"

The Conflict Widens

The problem of Constitution versus Bible involves more than just a few laws that happen to go against the laws of God. If it were a matter of one or two laws, we would simply ignore the few and obey the rest. But to give any earthly document the authority belonging only to the Word of God goes totally against the spirit of the first commandment. Christians cannot give their *unconditional* support to any human system of laws.

So what do we do? Renounce our citizenship? Certainly not. For one thing, we're likely to find ourselves under a system vastly more hostile to Christianity than the one we live with. China and her mandatory abortion laws are only one example.

The Constitution of the United States is possibly the best document of its kind ever devised. But this doesn't help us avoid a disturbing fact: We are embroiled in a complicated dilemma when we study the Ten Commandments in the seemingly contradictory light of Romans 13. And we haven't even gotten past the first commandment.

We can handle the second with little difficulty: "You shall not make for yourself an idol" (Exod. 20:4, *NASB*). Most of us have few problems avoiding graven images, though many will suggest that we actually worship the images of our material possessions, like our Corvettes, our luxury appliances, and our multi-story townhouses.

But when we get to the third commandment, "You shall not take the name of the Lord your God in vain" (Exod. 20:7, *NASB*), we are in trouble again. For many will insist it is vain to use God's name in our pledge of allegiance. We say, "one nation under God," while many of the policies we pledge to support are in bold defiance of God's laws! And surely it is vain to print the words "In God We Trust" on our money, when "In Thee We Trust" would tell the truth. Starting with her own currency, our nation trusts in everything *but* God!

Dual Allegiance Is Unworkable

We can see that no simple method of arranging a dual allegiance is ever going to present itself. On the one hand we have our allegiance to God, and on the other, our allegiance to the Constitution of the United States, which is our "governing authority." Jesus said, "No one can serve two masters" (Matt. 6:24, *NASB*). And we can see He is right. Dual allegiance is unworkable. But that is precisely what seems to be required of us when we contrast

Romans 13 either with the first commandment or with Peter's statement, "We must obey God rather than men."

Many Jews Were Anarchists

So why did Paul give us these confusing instructions? Why didn't he say, "Obey only God's laws, for His authority is higher than that of any earthly king or kingdom"? One reason is that the Jews, in Paul's time, were notoriously rebellious. Paul was addressing a people who, in their relation to the Roman government, were often virtual anarchists. They regarded no man as their king, only God. And for these volatile firebrands, passive resistance wouldn't do. The sort of violence and treachery we see every day in the Middle East had been second nature to the Jews for centuries before Paul's time. Assassination and murder were the Jewish answers to Roman rule, and Paul was clearly not in favor of bringing a tradition of violence and terrorism into the church of Jesus Christ.

Romans 13 Is for Today

But it just won't do to brush off Paul's instructions as though they were intended only for the Jews of the first century. Paul was making a point about Christian citizenship that applies not only to the Roman Christians, but to all Christians in all times. He knew that human systems of government, no matter how flawed, are preferable to anarchy. Paul intended for Christians to be model citizens. He expected the church to be the cornerstone of civic order and stability.

Our Hope Is in Christ

Paul does not mean that man-made systems of law and order are so good and so godly that for this reason it would always be wrong to revolt against them. What he does mean is this: The most appropriate way of expressing our hope as Christians is to abandon all thoughts of revolution. Our hope is set on Christ and His kingdom, not on any worldly order of things. And that's why Jesus said, "If My kingdom were of this world, then My servants would be fighting, that I might not be delivered up to the Jews" (John 18:36, *NASB*). To set our hope on Christ is to put aside every other consideration (especially our egos) and follow His example of sacrificial service.

PART II: THE ANSWER: DO AS JESUS DOES

Whoever understands the meaning of sacrificial service has the answer to the mystery we are trying to unravel: the answer is found in total, undivided devotion to Christ, in radical, uncompromising discipleship.

According to the nineteenth chapter of John, Jesus found Himself a prisoner in the hands of the Roman governor, Pilate. "Do you not know," Pilate asked, "that I have authority to release You, and I have authority to crucify You?" Jesus answered, "You would have no authority over Me, unless it had been given you from above" (John 19:10,11, *NASB*).

Here we see that Jesus agreed with the most important part of Paul's words on civic duty, "There is no authority except from God, and those which exist are established by God."

What About Hitler?

But now we must interrupt ourselves. A serious question arises that we cannot sidestep: "Did God establish the power of *all* governments? Even Hitler? And Soviet Russia? And the Ayatollah Khomeini?"

This question may be broken into two parts: (1) Why does God tolerate evil in the world and (2) Why does God specifically tolerate or apparently even establish governments that are thoroughly evil?

Christianity answers the first part of the question this way: (1) God is good. (2) He made all things good and for the sake of their goodness. (3) One of those good things was the free will of mankind. (4) Free will, by its very nature, may be abused. It therefore includes the possibil ity of evil. (5) Mankind has abused its free will and has become evil. (6) Since mankind persists in being evil, laws must be established to keep in check the behavior of those who present a danger to everyone else.

That's why we have drunk-driving laws. And laws against stealing. And international laws that protect one country from the aggression of another. The only alternative is anarchy. For this reason God allows us to establish systems of government, which we wouldn't need if we didn't choose to be evil.

As for people like Hitler or Khomeini, they clearly are openly and violently evil. They present an unusual threat to society, though their particular wickedness is essentially no different from anyone else's. They enjoy God-given free will just like the rest of us. But they have abused it, along with the political power their free will has brought them.

God does not remove free will from the world whenever someone like Hitler abuses it. If He did, it would be immediately and permanently removed; no one would have the power of making his or her own decisions. For at any given moment there is someone, somewhere, who is abusing that power. Of course we all abuse it to some extent. To remove free will would be to make all our actions merely inevitable, like gravity or the sunrise.

No Revolt Led by Christ

Now let's go back to what Jesus says about the government. Many have read Christ's words and concluded that He was condoning rebellion when He said to Pilate, "You would have no authority over me, unless it had been given you from above" (John 19:11, *NASB*). But just the opposite is true. Just a few hours earlier Jesus had said, "Do you think that I cannot appeal to My Father, and He will at once put at My disposal more than twelve legions of angels" (Matt. 26:53, *NASB*).

So not only did Jesus refuse to revolt against the Roman government (much to the chagrin of the politically-minded reactionaries of His day), He made it clear that revolt was unnecessary. For if revolt was ever called for, God would intervene and take care of it Himself.

False Chivalry

But this is a hard pill to swallow. Didn't we just say that sacrificial, radical discipleship is the key to solving our dilemma? And when we hear these words, don't we tend to think of "sacrificial" rebellion or martyrdom? It all sounds very heroic and chivalrous. But chivalry, as we have come to know it, is characterized by a sort of bravery that makes surprisingly cozy friends with cowardice. What we call bravery is often little more than egocentric pride, refusing to be thought of as submissive or weak. Males are especially prone to this kind of false bravado. They detest anything that smacks of submission or weakness. "I'm a man," they say, "and I'll go down fighting!"

Foolish Pride

But this kind of fighting spirit is found in both men and women. So those who have any point of contention with the government had better examine their motives closely to detect any traces of it. Are they looking for ways to rationalize their refusal to be thought of as weak? Of course nowadays we use the word *wimpy*.

Because we are proud, we like to identify with Peter. We, too, would make the bold announcement, "We must obey God rather than men." We cheer and say, "Way to go Peter! You showed 'em! They can only push us so far and then they'll see what we're *really* made of! We're men, not wimps!"

Taking It Literally

Our pride would keep us from taking Romans 13 literally. But Jesus, by His own example, has shown us the extent that we should do so. Yes, there are times when we must disobey the government in order to fully obey God. But if we harbor the least trace of pride, we have lost everything we might have gained by it. In fact, if we hope to gain personally by it at all we are only fooling ourselves.

Sometimes sincere compassion compels us to disobey the government. This was certainly the case with Corrie Ten Boom and her family, who hid Jews from the Nazis during World War II. But they did so with meekness, something that is foreign to many of us. Jesus' own example of meekness is familiar enough. Still, we find it difficult to follow. On the one hand we read Romans 13, and on the other we read the defiant words of Peter and Daniel. But we hear only what we want to hear. If we choose to disobey the government it's likely to be out of deference to our pride, our deadly selfish desire to look strong and brave and to avoid the appearance of being easily pushed around.

Our Pride Is Deadly

Pride is the deforming and enfeebling influence that

makes the world go 'round in such a sick, lopsided fashion. Pride brought about Lucifer's fall from heaven. "Better to reign in hell," he says, in Milton's *Paradise Lost*, "than serve in Heav'n." Out of pride the first man and woman rejected paradise and chose disobedience. And the same hell-inspired notion misguides men and women in the twentieth century. It destroys marriages and starts world wars. And its influence is formidable as we respond to Romans 13. For many will disobey the government, claiming to obey their consciences, when in fact they are only obeying their pride.

Some, of course, make no pretenses about conscience. They defy the government merely for convenience' sake. This is often the true reason for evading military service. Some break the law in order to save themselves money. They cheat on their income tax (or refuse to pay it altogether), and feel no shame whatever in doing so. But we have our hands full addressing those who at least *suppose* themselves to be following their consciences. To those who make no such claims we have nothing to say. They would profit little by it if we did.

When Should We Disobey?

We still haven't answered the question of exactly where Christians ought to draw the line between duty to God and duty to the government. How should Christians respond to a government that is entirely corrupt, a government that commands its citizens to act in ways that blatantly contravene the laws of God?

Jesus' Answer

Jesus answers these questions by appealing to the conscience. This, in fact, is something He spends a good deal of time talking about. We will use two of Jesus' statements to sum up our discussion on conscience. In Matthew 9:13 He quotes the Old Testament: "I desire compassion," He says, "and not sacrifice" (*NASB*). By sacrifice, Jesus means all the Jewish Law. But compassion, too, is one of God's laws. It also must be obeyed, and those who have genuine compassion, like the Ten Booms, need no one to tell them when to use it.

In Luke 12:57, Jesus poses a challenging question: "Why do you not even on your own initiative judge what is right?" (*NASB*). He refers here to the settling of civil disputes out of court. But He is addressing a mind-set common to all of us. And it comes up whenever we grapple with any apparent contradiction, such as the one we find between Romans 13 ("Be in subjection to the governing authorities") and Acts 5:29 ("We must obey God rather than men").

We Are All Like Pharisees

The problem with Romans 13 and its counterparts is simply that the vast majority of us, like the Pharisees, are looking for rigid, black and white rules. Because mere rules leave the conscience undisturbed. And awakening the conscience is dangerous business; it makes high and strenuous demands on us that we are slow to meet. It takes us far beyond the limits of written laws, and it may get us into hot water with both religious and secular authorities. And why not? For this is precisely what happened to Jesus.

It's no wonder we'd rather observe a rigid and predictable system of rules. That's the easy way to go. It requires only the lowest, pharisaical ways of thinking. But a healthy conscience, inspired by the Holy Spirit, requires a heart like Christ's.

A New Question of Motive

The Pharisees in Jesus' time were caught up in the minute letter of Jewish law. This law was carried out not for the love of God but for the love of appearing to be religious. And for the purpose of avoiding personal blame. This brings us to an entirely new problem.

The problem is this: We all tend to have a low regard for Scripture. That is, we are slow to understand that the Bible was given as a means of knowing our heavenly Father and all the things that please Him. Instead, and sadly, we often think of it as a means of escaping from Him. Rather than draw close to God, the Pharisee seeks protection *from* God in a set of legal contrivances in which God has somehow allowed Himself to be caught.

And with this we have opened a real can of worms. But it is a can that must be opened. For we must ask ourselves a difficult question if we are to get any further with Romans 13: If the most "religious" of us wish to avoid violating this part of Scripture, is it because we want to please God, doing only what is good, or because we wish to "stay out of trouble" with God at all costs?

A Motivation of Fear or Love?

Jesus comments on this attitude in His parable about stewardship in Matthew 25. A servant was given one talent, which he was expected to put to good use on behalf of his master. But instead, he buried it for safekeeping, out of fear. "I knew you to be a hard man," he explained later, "I was afraid and went away and hid your talent in the ground" (Matt. 25:24,25, *NASB*).

This servant was more concerned with staying out of trouble than with doing his duty. He was expected to make something of what he had been given, to invest it and show a profit. But he squandered an important opportunity because all he knew how to do was play it safe. And because he was afraid of losing what little he had, he lost even that. The one talent was taken away from him and he was left with nothing.

What paltry service we give to God if we act like that servant! How sad it must make Him when we obey Him merely to secure our own safety! In the military, people who care only for their own safety are called cowards. God does not want self-serving, hollow gestures of obedience. He wants us to know who He is, to love Him for it, and to obey Him because our hearts will settle for nothing less. He wants us to be like Christ, who was willing to suffer and die and take false blame for compassion's sake.

Christ's compassion is the best answer we have to our dilemma of church versus state. That dilemma looks much simpler in light of the following incident: Jesus had to make a choice: Should He heal a man on the Sabbath, a day when Jewish law allowed no work of any kind? Of course He should. And He did. But the Pharisees were concerned about this apparent breach of Sabbath law. So Jesus said, "What man shall there be among you who shall have one sheep, and if it falls into a pit on the Sabbath, will he not take hold of it, and lift it out? Of how much more value then is a man than a sheep! So then, it is lawful to do good on the Sabbath" (Matt. 12:11,12, *NASB*).

And did Jesus come to dismantle the laws of Moses and the Prophets? Jesus Himself answers, "I did not come to abolish, but to fulfill" (Matt. 5:17, *NASB*). And He did fulfill them, with His perfect knowledge of the law and His perfect obedience to its spirit. If we would be His disciples, Jesus would have us obey Romans 13 by all possible means, within the context of total, sacrificial obedience, obedience of the sort Jesus Himself practiced daily.

There is no formula that will enable us to draw a firm,

black line between God's laws and human laws. There is no system that will show us when we are bound to obey the government and when we are bound to obey only God. But God has given His Holy Spirit, along with an instrument to hear Him with, the conscience. He expects us to listen to Him, and He holds us accountable:

"Why do you not even on your own initiative judge what is right? (Luke 12:57, *NASB*). God wants us to let the Holy Spirit guide us into genuine devotion to Him, doing everything in our power to imitate Christ. Under no other circumstances may we say with Peter, "We must obey God rather than men."

11

Nuclear War

John Hambrick

Vapor. That's what we will be if somebody decides to use one of the world's tens of thousands of nuclear devices. Because nuclear bombs are like potato chips: it's hard to eat or use just one. If somebody fires one off, you can bet that whoever is being fired at is going to shoot one back, that is if they have one. Of course, that would be the last thing that you'd bet on, unless you decided to bet on whose hair was going to fall out first.

Any way you look at it, a nuclear war is not going to be much fun. In fact, it would be so awful that everyone, whether liberal or conservative, Democrat or Republican, agrees that we should try our best not to have one. The only problem is that we can't seem to agree on what is our best bet for avoiding a nuclear war.

Even among people who claim to be followers of Jesus Christ, there are all sorts of opinions as to what we should or should not do. Things get so intense between some of these Christians, that sometimes you hear one of them saying, "A *real* Christian couldn't possibly hold that position." Of course, there are some ideas about nuclear war which obviously could not be held by a Christian. For example, it's probably safe to say that a real Christian would never advocate letting the Democrats use a nuclear bomb to blow up Republicans, or vice versa. But those types of positions are pretty obvious. It's not a good idea to go around labeling a position about nuclear weapons as non-Christian unless it is obviously off the wall.

So, we won't be doing much labeling in this chapter. We won't attempt to label any of the positions we'll be discussing as right or wrong. But we will proceed along the following lines. In a few years you are going to be running this country. Some of you will be elected to public office. Some of you will be in a position to influence a lot of people. All of you, except you felons (you know who you are), will be able to vote. And those of you who are Christians will be expected, even commanded (see Col. 3:17), to exercise the above responsibilities in the name of Christ, attempting to bring Him honor by doing those things which please Him. And this even includes the position you endorse regarding the use of nuclear weapons. It wouldn't be much help to you if we were to try to pick out *the* Christian position for you. And anyway, that would be impossible because: (a) the author of this chapter isn't that smart; (b) it's not all that clear even to those people who are that smart. So instead, we will attempt to outline some facts and positions which will help you to come up with *your* position, one which you feel will please our Lord. And remember, He never told us to define *the* Christian position on anything. He just told us to follow Him.

WHAT IF THEY HAD A NUCLEAR WAR AT YOUR HOUSE?

To start things off, we want to help you visualize what would happen if somebody dropped an atomic bomb right over your house. Admittedly, you don't have to have a Ph.D. in physics to figure out that your house is going to be totalled, along with most of the neighborhood, not to mention most of the city. But unfortunately, it goes much further than that. For starters, every building within a mile and a half of your house (that's a circle with your house at the center and a three mile diameter) would be completely vaporized. No more school buildings, no more supermarkets, no more movie theaters. Everything would be gone. Within that circle, 98 percent of the people present at the time of the blast would be killed instantly. If you live on a farm which is pretty far away from everyone else, then maybe that would include only a few people. If you live in Los Angeles, New York, or London, that could mean that millions would die.

This circle we've been talking about is called the immediate blast zone. Outside the immediate blast zone many buildings would still be gutted. They just wouldn't be totally vaporized like your house. This partial destruction would happen up to three and a half miles from your house, or another two miles beyond the total destruction zone. Within this larger circle many would still be killed. In fact, people would suffer third degree burns (those are the really serious kind) up to 6 miles away from your house. That includes a circle with a diameter of 12 miles.

And have we mentioned the effects of radiation yet?

As a matter of fact, we haven't. Radiation is a mysterious thing. You can't see it, smell it, or feel it. It isn't hot or cold. In fact, you can't even tell if you've been exposed to radiation. That's why they wear those radiation detecting badges at nuclear power plants. But radiation could kill more people than the actual explosion. It is sort of like a tremendously potent poison. And it can be carried by the wind. Now, are you ready for the bad news about radiation? (And you thought you'd already heard it.) The bad news about radiation is that it can last for a long, long time. Tomorrow at school, ask your chemistry teacher what the half-life of plutonium is. They only deal with half lives because whole lives are too ridiculously long.

We aren't trying to depress you. We aren't trying to scare you either. We are just trying to get you to think about the terrible destruction a nuclear bomb can bring. And while we're at it, think about this. In an all-out nuclear war, the experts estimate that over 75 percent of all communities in the United States with populations of more than 25,000 would be hit by bombs that are many times more powerful than those that were dropped during World War II.

Jesus has assigned us a rather important task. He told us that we are the salt of the earth (Matt. 5:13). One of the functions of salt in biblical times was to act as a preservative. In other words, Jesus has called us to help preserve the society in which He has allowed us to live. And among other things, that includes attempting to help our society avoid a nuclear war. This is not a liberal thing. It's not a conservative thing. It doesn't mean we automatically become a Democrat or a Republican. Don't let people put you into a box over this. It is still true that peoples' eternities are of top priority. But perhaps the most tangible way we can show the world that we are concerned about their eternity is to show that we are concerned about the quality of their life in this world. Biblically, it is inconsistent to care about the one thing without caring about the other. If you will look up 1 John 4:19-21, you'll see that it says that we can't claim to love God if we don't also love people. And loving people demands that we be concerned about their earthly circumstances (see 1 John 3:17). So, being concerned about nuclear war isn't a non-spiritual thing. It is a direct result of trying to obey Jesus Christ. And *that* is about as spiritual as you can get.

THE ALTERNATIVES

Now it's time to talk about the ways different people have thought about stopping nuclear war. And remember, maybe you will never have your finger on one of those infamous buttons that launch a missile. But you will be in a position to influence the thinking of those people's bosses when election time rolls around.

As we mentioned earlier, there are tens of thousands of nuclear bombs in the world right now. You have, no doubt, been wondering why there are so many. After all, if one good-sized bomb could almost flatten a city like Washington, D.C. then how many bombs do we or our enemies really need? Just a few hundred bombs could wipe out almost every major city in the world. And even if one makes allowance for losing a few hundred to somebody's defense system, we would still have thousands of bombs left over. So, why so many? Well, it all has to do, believe it or not, with our efforts to avoid an all-out nuclear war. It is an anti-war strategy called M.A.D. M.A.D. stands for *Mutually Assured Destruction*. The idea is that in the event of a nuclear war, so many bombs would be launched, fired, and dropped, that even the winner would be almost totally destroyed. And of course, if the winner is going to lose almost as badly as the loser, then both sides are going to think twice about starting anything. In other words, because the destruction of both sides would be *mutually assured,* then both sides, because of the presence of all these bombs, will be less likely to start a nuclear war.

Some people don't like this strategy. They usually point out that in pursuing M.A.D. we are committed to spending a lot of money on weapons when we could be using the money to be doing good things like feeding starving people. They also mention that as more and more bombs are built, things get more and more tense.

Now there are two sides to the debate over M.A.D. as an effective deterrent against nuclear war. And please remember, we're not trying to push one side or the other. We are trying to provide you with some facts so that *you* can make a decision.

Here are some things which the people who advocate M.A.D. like to mention. First of all, they point to M.A.D.'s track record. Like it or not, M.A.D. is pretty much the strategy which has been in effect in recent history. And M.A.D.'s proponents point out that it has worked. We are still here. No nuclear bombs have been dropped as instruments of war since World War II.

Second, the people behind M.A.D. say that it is the only way to avoid nuclear war which takes into account the realities of human nature. They say that it would be nice if people were rational enough to dismantle all their nuclear weapons because they realized how destructive they are. And it would be nice to trust that they would leave them dismantled. But history shows time and again that people in general just aren't that rational. So, because we can't trust our powers of reasoning to steer us away from nuclear war, we have to resort instead to threats of retaliation. And the only threat big enough to discourage someone from using a nuclear bomb is another nuclear bomb. Thus, all the Russians' bombs will keep us from using our bombs, and all our bombs will keep the Russians from using theirs.

We hope that at this point you are a little confused. It's not that we like you to be confused. It's just that the arguments for and against M.A.D. are both pretty good. So if you have understood both sides of the issue then you are probably a bit unsure of what to think because they both seem to make sense. So, are you confused? Good. So are we. Let's go on then to some other ideas about how to avoid a nuclear war. In each case we will try to mention some arguments for and against the position in question.

When was the last time you saw a movie with guns in it? Maybe it was a western, or maybe it was a Star Wars type of film. If guns were in it, chances are there came a point in the movie where either the good guy or the bad guy told someone to drop their gun. They probably said something very creative, very Hollywood. After all, those writers are pretty clever. They probably wrote a dialogue which went something like this: "OK, drop your gun." (Wow.) At that point in the movie a disarmament has occurred. *Disarmament* is another popular idea which many people think will help us to avoid a nuclear war. Proponents of this theory are usually referring to one of two different kinds of disarmament; unilateral disarmament, or multilateral disarmament. While the two ideas are closely related, there are some important differences.

Unilateral disarmament occurs when one country with nuclear weapons chooses to get rid of them, regardless of whether or not its enemies decide to disarm. It is a one-sided action (hence *uni*lateral). People who support this theory think that the idea of a country laying down its nuclear weapons would be such a powerful example of trust and goodwill, that it would move other countries to do the same thing. Christians who support this idea note that it comes very close to following the principles which Jesus taught in the Sermon on the Mount. In Matthew 5:38,39 He says, "You have heard that it was said, 'Eye for eye, and tooth for tooth.' But I tell you, Do not resist an evil person. If someone strikes you on the right cheek, turn to him the other also."

Critics of unilateral disarmament, some of whom also happen to be Christians, say that the ethics which Jesus taught in the Sermon on the Mount were intended for Christian individuals to follow, not whole nations. They also say that such a position fails to take into account that some people will miss the positive example of unilateral disarmament and will see only a nuclearly unarmed country where there used to be a formidable foe.

The second kind of disarmament is multilateral disarmament. This is where two or more countries with nuclear weapons lay down or at least begin to lay down their nuclear weapons at the same time. In order for this type of thing to work, officials of the countries involved must sit down together and draw up some sort of a treaty. Among other things, this treaty must spell out a means by which the reductions can be verified. This is to prevent any cheating. The people who support this approach point out that treaties are a very common means of agreement between countries. They also mention that it doesn't call for one country to become vulnerable to a nuclear attack the way a unilateral plan does. The critics of multilateral disarmament like to point out that no matter what kind of anti-cheating measures a treaty would produce, it is still going to be next to impossible to really check out whether or not some country is merely hiding their bombs. And so,

with this in mind, we come to our last alternative and perhaps the most imaginative.

When George Lucas made the first Star Wars movie
back in the late seventies, who would have guessed that
the name he coined would soon be used to describe a
futuristic means of making nuclear war obsolete? Star
Wars isn't just a movie any more. Today it is a plan which
involves a system of satellites in space which will be used
to render nuclear devices inoperable. Its official name is
Strategic Defense Initiative (SDI).

The system, still very much in the planning stages, will
fire one of two things at the targets. One team of scientists is working on developing a thing called a smart rock.
These are special types of projectiles which travel so fast
that they can hit a nuclear device in a matter of seconds
and knock it out of commission by virtue of the smart
rock's great speed, without causing enough of an explosion
to trigger the nuclear bomb. Other scientists are working
on a laser system which can be fired at a nuclear device
and again put it out of commission without triggering a
nuclear blast. The idea is that either smart rocks or laser
beams will be put on these satellites. Should our enemies
fire a nuclear device at us, these defensive weapons,
guided by a very sophisticated radar system, would
destroy the missile, plane, or other weapon before it even
got close to us. In fact, they have already begun to work
on some of these devices with the space shuttle program.
The experts figure that even though we have the ideas, it
will be a long time before we actually have the technology
to make them work. But even so, it appears that some day
this science-fiction sounding option could actually help us
avoid a nuclear war.

But like the other alternatives, Star Wars has its critics. For one thing, the critics of Star Wars say that it is too

expensive. They say that it would cost billions of dollars to produce. That figure is correct. The debate is whether or not that is too high a cost for what Star Wars will actually produce. Star Wars critics also object to the idea of making space into a battle ground. They are worried that if we put weapons in space, that will make a nuclear war more likely rather than less so. And the last thing that critics of Star Wars, say is that developing the technology to make the whole system work will take too long. They think that by the time we have it working and in place our enemies will have found a way to get around it.

On the other hand, the people who support Star Wars like to point out that with this type of defensive system we don't have to depend on lengthy treaty negotiations nor on the integrity of some governments which we're not really sure we can trust. They also mention that, as in past situations, a project which is being developed for the military will also result in all sorts of nifty ideas for non-military use. Who knows? Maybe that's where we got frisbees and silly putty.

THE BALL IS IN YOUR COURT

So there you have it. We've told you a bit about the problem. Then we went on and outlined the various ways in which people have suggested that we can avoid a nuclear war. We also mentioned some of the pros and cons behind each idea. So now it's test time. Can you remember the four alternative suggestions to avoiding a nuclear war? You can? Good. Tell us what they are.

Yes, that's right. M.A.D. stands for Mutually Assured Destruction. And you remembered the two types of disarmament; unilateral and multilateral. Now what's the last one? No, not Star Trek. It's Star *Wars*. And how about the arguments for and against each position?

Jesus said, "Blessed are the peacemakers, for they will be called sons of God" (Matt. 5:9). He doesn't expect you to single-handedly change the world. He doesn't expect you to have all the answers. But He does expect you to care. He wants you to care about the world which He has entrusted to our care (see Gen. 1:28). He wants you to care about the other people in the world whom He loves very much, even if most of them don't even know Him. He wants you to care enough to take the time to think about nuclear war and how to avoid it. So take the time. Get familiar with the facts. This little chapter is just a start. But you can use it to help yourself begin to have an opinion. And remember, sometimes Christians are frantically searching for God to intervene in a miraculous fashion, in order to rescue us from our problems. And sometimes He does that. But if you study the Scriptures, you will find that isn't what He usually does. He usually works through His people. And that's where you come in.

12

If I Should Die Before I Wake

Ed Stewart

Tracy was a beautiful seventeen-year-old, a popular student and a talented competitor on her school's tennis team. In the summer following her junior year, Tracy attended a weekend water ski trip with her church youth group. She had just stepped out of the water from her turn on the skis when she complained of feeling faint. Within minutes she collapsed unconscious on the beach. As her family and friends tried frantically to wake her, Tracy's pulse and breathing stopped. Paramedics attempted to revive her, but Tracy was dead. The exact cause of death was never determined.

Bob was a sheriff's deputy in our county, a husband, and a father of a six-year-old girl. About four A.M. one winter night as he was working the graveyard shift, Bob responded to a "hot" burglary call. While speeding to the scene his patrol car hit a patch of slippery pavement, careened off the road, rolled, and slammed into a power pole. Bob, who was alone in the car, was killed instantly. He was thirty-three.

Granny had been ill and senile in a nursing home for the last few of her eighty-two years. Penne, a granddaughter who had visited and cared for Granny faithfully, was informed one morning that Granny was on the verge of death. Corrective surgery was impossible due to her frailty. Penne, her husband and a few friends gathered at Granny's bedside as the fatal infection squeezed the last ounces of life from her. After two days Granny died peacefully in a coma.

Greg was a brilliant young man who graduated from the university and seminary with honors. While serving as an associate pastor, Greg encountered some unusual and complex physical problems which affected his mental equilibrium and provoked a separation in his marriage. A few days after his twenty-ninth birthday, Greg wrote farewell letters to his wife, two-year-old daughter, and parents, and then swallowed a lethal overdose of medication and died alone in his apartment.

Mike, age forty-three, was a respected psychiatrist who had pioneered some exciting innovations in therapy for the mentally disturbed. One morning Mike sat in his downtown office dictating to his secretary when, suddenly, one of his patients burst into the room. As the secretary watched in horror, the deranged man lifted a shotgun from under his coat and blew Mike away with several rounds fired at pointblank range.

Steve was an avid hunter and fisherman who had just started a new job as manager of a sporting goods store. He was sitting on the couch eating a cookie while his wife Jane was preparing dinner when he suddenly yelled out in pain and fell over on the couch. He was dead before the paramedics arrived. The autopsy revealed that three of the major arteries from the heart had exploded. Steve was only thirty-eight.

Kara was born by emergency Caesarian section six weeks prematurely after her mother had started hemorrhaging during a routine prenatal examination. Though strong enough to live under normal conditions, Kara had lost too much blood and her breathing was erratic at birth. She was placed on a respirator but all corrective efforts failed. Kara died after only one day of life.

A TIME TO DIE

Though you don't know the victims in these seven tragic-but-true scenarios, you are undoubtedly touched by the sadness of their stories. It's the sadness that everyone in the human family feels when we hear that one of our number has been taken from us. Death happens all around us every day, yet we never seem to get used to the newspaper stories, TV reports, letters or phone calls which announce someone's passing. And when the victim is a member of your family or circle of friends the pain is even greater. I know. In the paragraphs above, Tracy was our daughter's tennis teammate. Bob and Steve were personal friends of mine from our church (their deaths were only two weeks apart). Penne is another friend and I sat with her as Granny died. Greg and I served on the same pastoral staff for two and a half years. Mike attended a nearby sister church in our denomination. And Kara was our second daughter.

I'm not the only one who's had heart-ripping experiences with death. If you were writing this chapter, you would be able to tell your own sad stories—a parent who died while you were still a child, a friend killed in a car crash, or a grandparent quietly gone.

Death is a fact of life (see Eccles. 3:1,2; Heb. 9:27). And with each incident we hear about comes the sobering realization that none of us who have survived thus far is immortal. It could have been me pinned inside the patrol car. It could have been you crumpled and still on the lake shore. And some day, whether by injury, illness or "natural" causes, each one of us will die (unless the Lord returns first!). Some day you and I will be the victims that others will read about.

HARD QUESTIONS AND HEAVENLY QUIET

For all the fear and perplexity which His human creation suffers over the subject of death, God seems to be curiously quiet and unconcerned. My wife and I were torn up inside when Kara died. Didn't God hurt too? We couldn't tell. We were shocked to learn of Greg's suicide. Couldn't God have warned us in time to help him? If He did, we didn't hear Him. And it was so difficult to tell Bob's wife and daughter, "Everything will be okay," just hours after his broken body was pulled from the mangled patrol car. Wasn't God strong enough to keep that car on the road? He never told us why He chose not to prevent the crash.

Yes, the subject of death is tangled with many unanswered questions for those of us left behind. And many of the questions tempt us to doubt God's love and power. "If God is so loving," we argue, "why did He take a beautiful girl like Tracy for no apparent reason? If He is so powerful, why didn't he jam that shotgun pointed at Mike or hold Steve's heart together?" Perhaps for you the names and situations are different but the questions are painfully the same.

And what about the soul-probing questions we silently ask about our own deaths? When will I die? How will I die? What really happens at death? Will God really be there "on the other side"? We wake up each morning with no guarantee that we will live through the day or awaken tomorrow. Yet God is strangely silent about these details. Even wise Solomon could only conclude, "No man has power over the wind to contain it; so no one has power over the day of his death" (Eccles. 8:8).

The gnawing questions about death are sometimes like waves. They swell to such heights around us that they sweep us off our feet and we momentarily lose contact with solid ground. It sometimes appears to us that God has lost control in matters of life and death or that He is unconcerned. And it sometimes seems that our logical doubts make more sense than God's apparently illogical action (or lack of action).

But the truth of the matter is that God is a sovereign God. He gave life and He can take it away as He chooses (see Job 34:14,15). Furthermore, God does not need to answer to us for His actions or provide us an explanation for "untimely" deaths. Though the intrusion of death may be difficult to accept, and may cause questions we cannot answer and doubts we cannot quench, we must remember that somewhere beneath our feet is the bedrock surety that God is sovereign and just. Nothing happens to any of

His children without being thoroughly screened and approved by Him. Such truth should help us keep from drowning while riding out the stormy questions. The firmer the grip we have on God's sovereignty, the less trouble we will have with His silence.

LOOKING THROUGH GOD-COLORED GLASSES

Whenever God's view of something and your view of something don't match, guess whose view needs to change. Right, yours! God's perspective is eternally perfect and clear. Our perspective is frustratingly imperfect and cloudy. If we want to see things the way they really are—including the subject of death—we must attempt to look through God-colored glasses. We must continually attempt to move toward God's perspective. And when we do not see things exactly as He does, we must learn to be content with the knowledge that His perspective, though sometimes elusive, is perfect. He knows what He is doing—even in matters of life and death—when we cannot understand what He is doing.

We would probably agree that, from our limited perspective, there are many things about death we do not understand and even some things we fear. Where can we go to fill in the blanks in our perspective? Some accounts have surfaced recently from people who claim to have died, caught a glimpse of heaven, and returned to tell about it. Maybe so. But the primary source for God's perspective on any subject is the Bible. Though many of our questions about death may remain unanswered until we see the Lord face to face, the Bible provides enough information for us to acquire a healthy perspective of life's final event.

THE ULTIMATE BAD DAY

One of the saddest scenes I have ever witnessed occurred at the funeral of a man who was an unbeliever. His wife and grown children, also unbelievers, were understandably grief-stricken. As they gathered around the casket to pay their final respects, the family members wailed and sobbed uncontrollably, at times throwing themselves upon the lifeless corpse, knowing they would never see him again.

In our godless world which glibly wishes each other, "Have a nice day!", death is the ultimate bad day. In a humanistic society which is at best apathetic about death and at worst terrified and paranoid about it, staying alive is seen as the ultimate value. Medical science is feverishly dedicated to the preservation of life and prevention of death. (In some cases dead bodies are frozen in hopes that a cure for their fatal diseases will be discovered in time to unfreeze them, cure them and bring them back to life.) On the social scene, the death penalty is often seen by people as cruel and unusual punishment even for the most despicable crimes. And environmentalists are vigorously working to save the whales, seals, buffalo, and other endangered species. It is sadly ironic, however, that our culture's pro-life and anti-death stance breaks down when it comes to saving the most helpless of endangered species, the unborn human fetus!

For those without a saving knowledge of Christ, who grasp every passing minute because of the uncertainty of life after death, death *is* the ultimate bad day. For unbelievers death is a doorway which leads to a black, empty and foreboding unknown. For some, life, even with its daily futility and emptiness, is preferred over the uncertainty of the grave. For others, life is so bleak and hopeless that suicide—a self-initiated leap into the unknown chasm of death—is seen as a solution instead of a problem.

But what is God's perspective on the "ultimate bad day," the death of unbelievers? He apparently is not as concerned about preserving human life at all costs as we might think. After all, God has personally caused the deaths of innumerable godless individuals over the centuries of human history. The Old Testament graphically illustrates that God's trump card in the judgment of unrighteousness among His human creation is the death penalty.

When all but Noah and his family had turned their backs on Him, God drowned everyone who wouldn't climb on the ark (see Gen. 6-7). When Achan violated God's instructions about taking the spoils of the battle, God commanded that he and his family be stoned to death (see Josh. 7). When a nation of Amalekites angered God by mistreating Israel, his instructions were, "Totally destroy everything that belongs to them. Do not spare them; put to death men and women, children and infants, cattle and sheep, camels and donkeys" (1 Sam. 15:3).

The examples above don't exactly fit the picture we sometimes hold of God as the kindly grandfather who overlooks the misbehavior of bratty kids so He may shower them with candy. Yes, God is gracious, merciful and forgiving. But there comes a point at which He says, "You have had your chance, your sin must be punished, you are history." God is definitely not timid about judging unrighteousness by abruptly terminating the lives of those who oppose Him.

Thousands of unbelievers worldwide die each day from flood, famine, earthquake, tornado, war, accident, illness, and other fatal experiences. How many deaths are the result of God's immediate judgment on sin as in the case of the biblical examples above? And how many are the result of God indirectly allowing disease, violence, aging and natural law to run their courses unchecked? Perhaps that detail of God's perspective is still too fuzzy. Yet it remains that God causes and/or allows countless unbelievers to die without so much as a show of emotion.

But lest God be wrongly characterized as a heartless celestial mass killer, consider His words to Ezekiel: "I take no pleasure in the death of the wicked, but rather that they turn from their ways and live" (Ezek. 33:11). For God, the fact of death's certainty, be it directly or indirectly caused by Him, is a deterrent to unrighteousness and an encouragement to righteousness. And since His judgment is just and sure, we must reach out to unbelievers with compassion and haste to tell them of the mercy which is available from the God who will otherwise judge them.

THE VALUE OF DEATH

In contrast to the sad hopelessness of those who die without God, the Bible makes this interesting observation about the death of believers: "Precious in the sight of the Lord is the death of his saints" (Ps. 116:15). The word "precious" in this verse means heavy or weighty. It refers to the measurement of precious metals by weight. God is comparing the death of believers to the value of gold or silver.

Interestingly, we are not told *why* a believer's death is precious to God. Perhaps it is because death is a doorway through which all God's people must pass in order to enter intimate communion with Him for eternity. Presently our fellowship with God is limited by our humanity, by time and by space. But after death we are promoted into the spiritual realm unbounded by the restrictions of our human bodies. Our death may be valuable to God because it releases us to enjoy His presence even more than we can now.

Furthermore, the death of a believer may be valuable to God because of the impact it has on the relatives and friends of the one who has died. Someone once said that death is the greatest preacher in the world. The sobering loss of a loved one often causes people to think more seriously about God than they otherwise would.

Many high school students were more receptive to the gospel of Christ when they heard it proclaimed at their friend Tracy's funeral than they might have ever been before her death. Bob's funeral was attended by more than 200 uniformed policemen who heard the love of Christ proclaimed in sermon and eulogy. About 17 acknowledged a desire to receive Christ as Saviour at the close of the service. No wonder Bob's death was precious to God. It was the avenue through which several others came to life!

The apostle Paul summed up the perspective we need to adopt toward the death of believers with these lines: "If we live, we live to the Lord; and if we die, we die to the Lord. So, whether we live or die, we belong to the Lord" (Rom. 14:8); "Christ will be exalted in my body, whether by life or by death. For to me, to live is Christ and to die is gain" (Phil. 1:20,21). Death is not the ultimate bad day for the believer. Rather, it is just another element of our lives in which we can glorify God.

THE FEAR FACTOR

The story is told of two Puritans who met on the forest trail one Sunday morning while walking to church. One of the men was carrying a loaded musket and warily eyeing the brush around the trail. The other man said, "Brother, don't you realize that, when your time comes, you will die whether or not you have a musket to defend yourself?"

"Yes, brother, I know," the armed man said confidently.

"Then why do you carry a loaded musket?" the other man asked.

"Because, brother," the man with the musket replied, "I might meet a savage whose time has come."

A respectful fear of anything which may cause our death is natural and good. We all practice certain measures of safety and health so that we can prolong our lives. We wear seat belts, install smoke detectors, take vitamins and medicine, avoid contact with germs, obey traffic laws, and so on. There's nothing wrong with wanting to enjoy a meaningful, productive life and suspend our death for as long as possible.

As for me, I don't like riding motorcycles, working with household electricity, or being around guns because I am afraid of their life-ending capabilities. Other people avoid airplanes, swimming, heights and endless lists of supposed dangers for the same reason. Some of our fears and phobias are valid, some are not. But they all have their root in fearing a "premature" death.

Though I have some definite fears about the *way* I might die, I can honestly say that I am not afraid to die. My death is precious to God and ultimately good for me. Paul said he was torn between the choices of remaining alive to continue his ministry and dying to be with Christ, "which is better by far" (Phil. 1:23). David said, "Even though I walk through the valley of the shadow of death, I will fear no evil, for you are with me" (Ps. 23:4). Since God is the Lord of death as well as my Lord, death need not be feared as an enemy but may be welcomed as a friend. Whenever and however death occurs to me, I know that God will be

with me in it and that I will be even better off after I have
passed through it.

IN THE MEANTIME

So here we are. I'm still alive and typing and you're still
alive and reading. If you're a Christian like I am, you are
anticipating your eventual death with some fears and questions, but hopefully with a measure of confidence and perhaps even a trace of joy that Christ is preparing heaven's
unspeakable beauties for you to enjoy. If you are not a
Christian, I cannot offer you much hope concerning your
death until you open your life to God through a loving relationship with His Son Jesus Christ. Not only will Christ
provide you a hope in the face of death, but He will also
give you a purpose for the life you have yet to live before
death comes.

Since we can look forward to such a hopeful end to life,
the temptation may be to stay as comfortable as possible,
enjoy as much of life as possible, and coast our way into
Glory. But Solomon's instruction reveals God's perspective on how to occupy the remaining years, months,
weeks, or days of life: "Whatever your hand finds to do,
do it with all your might, for in the grave, where you are
going, there is neither working nor planning nor knowledge nor wisdom" (Eccles. 9:10). I hear Solomon saying
that real retirement comes *after* death, not before. While
we are alive we are to give ourselves wholeheartedly to
whatever work needs to be done.

For the Christian, all work is ministry-related—that is,
it involves loving God and loving people. There are hungry
people who need to be fed. There is injustice which needs
to be corrected. There is evil which needs to be con-
quered. And there are unbelievers around the world to

whom the message of hope in Christ needs to be taken.

We have more than enough to do to keep us busy for several lifetimes, but we are each allotted only one. With this fact in mind, Moses prayed a prayer we could all use: "Teach us to number our days aright" (Ps. 90:12). There is so much to do and so little time in which to do it, we need God's wisdom on how to schedule our time and make our remaining days as profitable as possible.

I am looking forward to a reunion with the seven people whose deaths I described in the opening paragraphs of this chapter. With the exception of newborn Kara and aged Granny, they were all involved in serving God with their days when death interrupted their activity. Tracy was an officer in her youth group. Bob was a coordinator of our children's church. Before his illness, Greg was a dedicated, conscientious minister. Mike had recently been baptized and was beginning an aggressive walk with the Lord. And Steve, a fairly new Christian, had just launched a ministry of producing Christian tapes for the visually impaired in our church.

None of these people was finished living—they all would have chosen to stay here longer. And we were not ready to let them go. But in the midst of the quandry, "Why them? Why now?" we were able to praise God and agree with the poet who wrote, "Only one life, 'twill soon be past; only what's done for Christ will last."